Lea

Ian Sanders has been 'doing it himself' for seven years as a business and marketing consultant. He has helped launch new ventures in radio, television, design and music. His current marketing company, OHM, (Outhouse Media), has clients that range from global brands such as Benetton to the small business around the corner.

Ian's skills are in bringing common sense advice and fresh perspectives to clients whatever their size, helping them to exploit their market potential. With more and more of his contacts setting up by themselves, Ian was inspired to write up his experiences in *Leap!* With his eight years as an independent and another ten years working for others, his mix of experience, insight and ideas makes him best placed to guide others through this new *scrambled up world of work*.

Ian is passionate about enterprise, about doing it differently and reinventing to succeed. He currently lives in Leigh-on-Sea with his wife, Zoë, and two children.

Leap!

Ditch your job, start your own business and set yourself free

Ian Sanders

CAPSTONE

Copyright © Ian Sanders 2008

First published 2008 by
Capstone Publishing Ltd. (a Wiley Company)
The Atrium, Southern Gate, Chichester, PO19 8SQ, UK.
www.wileyeurope.com

Email (for orders and customer service enquires): cs-books@wiley.co.uk

The right of Ian Sanders to be identified as the author of this book has been asserted in
accordance with the Copyright, Designs and Patents Act 1988

All Rights Reserved. No part of this publication may be reproduced, stored in a
retrieval system or transmitted in any form or by any means, electronic, mechanical,
photocopying, recording, scanning or otherwise, except under the terms of the
Copyright, Designs and Patents Act 1988 or under the terms of a licence issued by
the Copyright Licensing Agency Ltd, 90 Tottenham Court Road, London W1T 4LP, UK,
without the permission in writing of the Publisher. Requests to the Publisher should be
addressed to the Permissions Department, John Wiley & Sons Ltd, The Atrium, Southern
Gate, Chichester, West Sussex PO19 8SQ, England, or emailed to permreq@wiley.co.uk,
or faxed to (+44) 1243 770571.

Designations used by companies to distinguish their products are often claimed as
trademarks. All brand names and product names used in this book are trade names,
service marks, trademarks or registered trademarks of their respective owners. The
Publisher is not associated with any product or vendor mentioned in this book. This
publication is designed to provide accurate and authoritative information in regard to the
subject matter covered. It is sold on the understanding that the Publisher is not engaged
in rendering professional services. If professional advice or other expert assistance is
required, the services of a competent professional should be sought.

Other Wiley Editorial Offices: Hoboken, San Fransisco, Weinheim, Australia, Singapore and
Canada
Wiley also publishes its books in a variety of electronic formats. Some content that
appears in print may not be available in electronic books.

Library of Congress Cataloging-in-Publication Data
Sanders, Ian, 1968-
 Leap! : ditch your job, start your own business & set yourself free / by Ian Sanders.
   p. cm.
 Includes index.
 ISBN 978-1-84112-798-9 (pbk. : alk. paper)
 1. New business enterprises–Management. 2. Entrepreneurship. I. Title.
 HD62.5.S27155 2007
 658.1'1–dc22

                                                              2007039316

ISBN   978-184112-798-9

Set in Univers by Sparks (www.sparks.co.uk)
Printed and bound in Great Britain by TJ International Ltd, Padstow, Cornwall

This book is printed on acid-free paper responsibly manufactured from sustainable
forestry in which at least two trees are planted for each one used for paper production.
Substantial discounts on bulk quantities of Capstone Books are available to corporations,
professional associations and other organizations. For details telephone John Wiley &
Sons on (+44) 1243–770441, fax (+44) 1243 770571 or email corporatedevelopment@
wiley.co.uk

This is for Zoë, Barney and Dylan

Contents

Part Two: ENTERPRISE

Part Three: SUCCESS

Preface

I took the Leap to go it alone in 2000. It seemed appropriate making a landmark change in such a landmark year. A good time to start something new.

I felt like a pioneer then, changing my working life so radically. Now, eight years later, everybody seems to be doing it. The world is full of the self-employed: workers running businesses from spare rooms, attics and sheds. Go in to any coffee shop and you'll see people working at their laptops, many of them self-employed. But wherever they're based, what unites everyone is the desire to succeed, to be enterprising and to be self-sufficient.

Traditional business and the concept of a 'proper job' have changed as workers have sought to exploit the opportunities of the New Economy where it's a case of 'survival of the fittest'. In this new marketplace it seems you can do whatever you want, but competition has never been fiercer. Being successful is no longer about travelling in a flash car, in your flash suit to work in a flash office for a multinational corporation (thank goodness). It's all about *you*.

This is a world of no rules and no walls. Traditional trading barriers are down; the concept of bricks-and-mortar companies where employees go to work 9–5 is crumbling. The opportunities for the entrepreneur-within are huge. Welcome to *the scrambled up world of work*.

* * *

The idea for the book came in 2004 and I used a trip to Palo Alto, California to give me the inspiration to start writing it. Palo Alto is where a lot of Silicon Valley does their thinking. The town is close to Stanford University and has incubated many great business ideas from Facebook to Hewlett Packard. As I sat amongst the coffee shop entrepreneurs at the town's Printers Inc. café, it seemed a good place to start writing. But once I got back to the UK I became busy with plans for my latest business venture, and the book idea sat dormant. It was another trip away (you'll discover the importance of these later) in October 2006 when I had the time and the clarity to start the book again.

This book is a consolidation of my last eight years: shaping my experiences in that *scrambled up world of work* into some kind of order.

I've always been stimulated by the notion of creating something from nothing. From that small idea I had on a trip away to seeing this book published – it's satisfying taking an idea and a project to fruition. To make it a reality.

This book is both for those who've already gone it alone and those who are summoning up the courage to do it.

Visit my blog at www.scrambledupworld.com. My business ohm helps clients to exploit their market potential. If you're interested in working with me, please get in touch at talktous@ohmlondon.com.

Acknowledgements

Thanks to: Fiona Cummings for her support and encouragement; David Sloly and Richard Harrison for their ideas and feedback; Tim McQuaid for capturing the original idea on video; Pascal, Alex, Chris, Aki and Tonia for sharing their experiences on taking the *Leap!*; Adam Bennett at Hatstand for his quote; Simon Trewin for advice; Emma Swaisland and all the team at Capstone for their commitment to the project; George Hazlewood for spotting the missing 'r'; Tom Peters and Charles Handy for inspiration; Ugo's, Villa Cervarolo and Padre Aviles for thinking and writing places; Illy and Red Bull for stimulation; Zoë for her comments and suggestions.

Introduction

WHAT THIS ISN'T

Leap! isn't a book about how to set up a business, describing the nuts and bolts of what you need to do. It doesn't offer tax advice; it's not about financial planning, business plans or exit strategies. It offers no new theories on management success, no secret formula to make millions.

It's simpler than that. It's about the *approach* to a new way of working. About what you need to survive and succeed in the new world of business, in the *scrambled up world of work*.

WHO DO YOU THINK YOU ARE?

When you start your working life, few of us have a 'plan'. You get a job, work hard, do well and then, five or even ten years later, you wake up one day and say 'Hang on, I never meant to do this for *that* long.'

Change is rarely easy but is often liberating. Changing your work or business identity can be incredibly powerful in re-energizing your whole life. And working for yourself, whilst stressful and scary, can represent a whole new 'you'.

If you feel stale, bored or unfulfilled, quitting the 9–5 to do your own thing can help you rediscover yourself, to find the 'lost you' buried in the ten years of 9–5 drudgery.

Once you've decided to set up on your own or start your own business, you're going to need 'entrepreneurial spirit', and lots of it. Tenacity, drive, ambition, vision, patience, resolve – a whole box full of tools.

Think 'entrepreneur' and people think of successful business leaders who started small and made it big. But you don't have to lead a big company to be successful in business.

Being an entrepreneur is much simpler – and more critical – than all that. At its most basic, it's someone who pays him or herself from the proceeds of their own abilities. Someone who has the guts – and the vision – to create *something* from *nothing*. Someone who doesn't rely on a guaranteed pay cheque at the end of the month, but takes a risk to go the DIY route.

! An associate who left his job in a big music publishing company and started his own business. He's one.

! A friend from university who resigned her job as a staff writer and became a freelance journalist. She's one.

! A guy who left an IT job to set up a company managing bands. He's one.

! A woman who left her job working for a technology company and set up an interior design business online. She's another.

! A bloke who quit a mortgage company to start his own, very distinctive, one. He's another.

! A bloke I know who was made redundant and bought a window cleaning business. He's one.

! A mate quit working for a global brand and set up as a freelance copywriter. So is he.

They have all taken a risk.

And they all have their tools of the trade. Some work from home, others have offices. Some have a ladder and a bucket, others a database or a piece of software. Some just have their mobile phone and a bunch of contacts. But everyone has their intellectual capital and they each have an IDEA. Ideas for great products or services. Ideas for a different way of providing a traditional service. Ideas for innovative business models. And, with the right attitude and approach, *anyone* can do it.

In this new world of the entrepreneur you can do what you want, but if you do nothing then you get paid nothing. That might have been OK in your old job, coasting through quiet periods or leaving sales to those guys in the flash suits downstairs, but quiet times = quiet revenues.

So the biggest challenge is that you don't just have to do the work, you have to seek it out too. You have to hunt and win business before you can even 'do' business.

So welcome to a *scrambled up world of work*. It's hard work, there are no rules, it's survival of the fittest, but there are loads of opportunities out there.

Leap! navigates you through this *workscape* with four key areas to focus on for success:

1   Having the right ATTITUDE.

2   Applying an ENTERPRISING approach.

3   Knowing the tricks of the trade to be SUCCESSFUL.

4   Adjusting to your new WORKLIFE.

Part One
ATTITUDE

Before you quit and take that *Leap!* you need to be prepared. Not prepared in terms of stacks of research, focus group feedback, business plans, spreadsheets and projections. But prepared in a much more essential way.

You need the right kind of MINDSET. In your approach to work, in how you generate ideas, and what you think is important.

It's like a philosophy. It's an ATTITUDE.

1

Starting out

A blank screen, a blank page in a notebook or a blank canvas.
If faced with that blankness, it can be scary.
What to write?
How to start?
But then once you start, it's easy.
(Hey I am on line 6 already – see what I mean?)
And you always have to start somewhere.

To get the starting bit right you're going to need a lot of discipline and dedication. And you need to recognize that 'passive' is just not an option, so you'd better delete it from your vocabulary.

You've got to be constantly active, developing thoughts and plans, posing – and answering – a whole load of questions to yourself.

So before you do anything, before you *Leap!* you need to deal with the essentials. And then you can get started for real.

So ask yourself some questions:

! What do I really want to do with my professional life?

! What do I want to achieve?

! What will make me happy?

! What have I always wanted to do, but never done anything about?

! What is holding me back, what are the obstacles?

Lose those inhibitions and set some goals of what you want to achieve.

And once you have done that, you're already started.

2

Make sure you're hungry

If you are going to succeed in your *Leap!* you have to *want* success. You have to be hungry. Because if you're not, someone else will be. And that someone else is your competitor.

If you are only accountable to yourself, and especially if you work from home, then you have to be even hungrier, because it's going to take more discipline.

If you're lazy or want to do the bare minimum to be successful then forget it – it won't happen. If you're one of those people who like working in a company where you can turn up and hide behind your screen all day, pretending you are working hard, then listen very carefully:

1   Your
2   Days
3   Are
4   Numbered

Success is not the result of a half-hearted investment of time and effort. It's a commitment. It has to be all or nothing. A total 100% commitment or nothing at all.

That's not to say you can't balance multiple projects or even multiple businesses, or balance working with childcare. It just means your mental investment has to be absolute.

3

Passion wins

As well as your commitment, you have to be passionate about your business. If you've gone into an area of business because you think you can make money rather than because you have the passion for the product it will be tougher to succeed.

You may have identified a piece of software that you think will make you rich. But unless you really believe in it, live and breathe it, you might not have that passion. And passion will give you the edge. There's nothing worse than a salesperson giving a performance for a product you know they don't rate or love.

So you need to ensure that you have motives other than just wanting to make money when it comes to your business. Of course you don't need to have created the product itself to have the passion to sell it. I sell design-led solutions for clients but I'm no designer myself – I have designers who do those bits. But I'm passionate about the power of good design in business, about good branding and effective communications. I believe in that fiercely and could never sell something I don't believe in. Even if the client sector or subject matter is, on the face of it, 'boring', I make sure I get passionate about it. If I can't, it won't work. With every project, every brief, I get under the skin of the client and their target audience to make sure our ideas are effective and successful.

If you are stuck for 'The Idea' of what kind of business you want to start up, focus on what you are passionate about. What is your hobby or interest? What do you know a lot about? Because it's easier trying to sell a service in a sector you know lots about then trying to cold-call in one you know very little about.

Let your business be a reflection of your personality and your philosophy in an area you know lots about. Getting that bit right is a good step towards success.

4

Get known for being a safe pair of hands

Make sure you are a 'can do' kind of person, because you need to be a 'can do' business to succeed. Where competition is fierce and when you've just started out, 'can't do' will get you nowhere. Because clients like passing problems and challenges to suppliers who say 'we can do'. Your success in the relationship is about being able to take away the headache from the client.

And, similarly, you'll want to recruit those kind of people on your own projects. Because when you've won a piece of business or have a project to deliver you don't want your team to start saying they can't do things. Our budget was tightened on a project for a client. I asked my own supplier, 'Is it still feasible on the reduced budget?

'It's all do-able,' came the email back.

Music to my ears. And any client's ears. And that's why we have a relationship that works, why we have projects that deliver and clients who'll come back for more.

So get a reputation for someone who *does*, and aspire to be seen as a business that is *a good safe pair of hands*. Because whilst being a good safe pair of hands may not make you *Entrepreneur Of The Year*, it's what winning and retaining clients is all about.

5

Be distinctive

To win and retain business you need to be distinctive – and that means being different. Maybe in a superficial way: a fresh brand identity or website in a sector where all your competitors come across as boring. Or in a more intrinsic way: with a really unique offering, providing a bunch of services that no one else is providing under one roof.

I met a bloke who runs a small business locally, a company in the financial sector that does things differently. No suits. No stuffy offices. No conventional website.

A cool sofa instead of a boardroom table. An innovative customer referral initiative. An MD wearing flip-flops and shorts … in November. OK, at worst a bunch of gimmicks, but don't knock them – they are making an effort, they have a shedful of ideas, they have *balls* and they are out there. No reluctance to try new ideas, no lack of confidence for just getting out there and trying stuff. No ideas sitting getting dusty on the shelf – they are actually doing something about them, trying them all out with no fear of failure. Being pioneering and original in a sector full of stuffiness. No business school methodology, no marketing hot shots, just some damn good ideas.

Ten out of ten for guts.

6

Don't bullshit

Don't lie.

Whilst inevitably there's a lot of bullshit in business, don't deal with people who lie. Potential team members who lie about their achievements or clients who lie about their commitment. In a world where trust is so important to business relationships, steer clear of bullshit. Be honest in communications, in pitches and meetings. Don't bullshit your achievements, abilities or credentials. At worst your lies will be obvious because you cannot back something up; or it may sound like a load of arrogant bravado.

I had dealings with this guy who promised me this meeting and that project, saying he had emailed me when he hadn't; saying I had said something when I hadn't and it all got a bit tedious. When it comes to you and your business, lying will get you a bad reputation or you'll get found out – or both.

A colleague told a few white lies in a job interview, that he'd been responsible for something that was his boss's achievement. That might seem innocent but it's a small world and his little lie could easily be disclaimed. In a single phone call it could all crumble. Sure, you need to choreograph your career history, to spin it in the most positive way, but don't jeopardize your reputation.

You need to get known for your reputation and being decent in business. Because there are lots of sharks out there and it pays to offer the tell-it-like-it-is, bullshit-free solution. Clients will find that refreshing.

You are the brand. Your reputation and your intellectual capital is all there is.

Don't mess it up.

7

Perception is everything

First impressions count. That first meeting, that first phone call, that first email, that first proposal. Make sure that first impression is the best impression you can give because that's what clients will remember. How you greeted the client, that handshake, the eye contact – all those parts of your body language are important.

As are your business communications. Whilst you want to stay clear of bullshit, remember the importance of perception. A website that punches above its weight in terms of style and professionalism = good; a website that bullshits about numbers of staff or lies about clients = bad.

You want to be the market leader?
Then act like the market leader.

In my early 20s I walked into a new job. The role was junior but I liked the company and figured (rightly) it was a good place to grow. So I took the job. The guy that hired me reminded me I was going to be the lowest paid member of staff there and I would not get a pay-rise for a while. I took the risk and walked into the job as the lowest paid, newest recruit. But I didn't act like that. I wore a tie every day*, I took the initiative and generated board papers, came up with ideas without being asked. I think everyone thought I was more important than I was meant to be. Within five months I was promoted and within five years I was a director of the company and earning six times my entry salary.

Sure I had some ups and downs along the way but I was successful because of the attitude I had on day one; and that attitude influenced perception.

So act the part. Or at least act the part you want to play.

8
Soaking it up

When you are setting up your own business, you need to be a sponge.

---

*And I haven't worn a tie since I took the *Leap!*

Your ideas and your values are a direct result of what you see and experience, what inspires and stimulates you. And so you have to feed your brain, give it material to soak up.

There's so much material out there to consume, sometimes it's difficult to know where to start. Do loads of research on your target market, read other people's stories on business. Keep a cuttings file on entrepreneurs and start-ups, check out relevant TV and radio shows, search online.

And don't stop.

Books. Blogs. Websites. Newspapers. Magazines. Go out of your comfort zone. Pick up a magazine or read a paper you'd never normally look at. For instance, read *The Financial Times*, the *New Scientist or Marketing Week*.

Scribble all over it, make notes, have thoughts.

It will take you in directions you hadn't even thought of, open your eyes to new possibilities and new ways of doing things.

You have to be open to different voices and views; don't just stick with what you know, stick your neck out and soak up that stuff you didn't know.

You'll find it triggers results.

9

Warning: steep incline ahead

I've just written a report on an industry I didn't know much about. I had a quick turnaround on it. Two days to produce it. I knew very little about the subject before I started. Now I know a lot. The client commissioned me because he wanted my clarity and insight, skills that he saw as transferable whatever the subject matter.

I sweated. I engrossed myself in the subject matter. I shut myself away for two days, started early and worked late. I sat at my desk doing research, then lay on the floor and made scribbles on paper. I lived and breathed another industry. Now I know lots (not everything); but I knew enough to write a damn good report. Just think what I could have done with four days or ten days.

It was a stimulating journey – a finite project with a beginning and an end. And now it's gone. It was quick and I had no choice but to fast-track my learning. Five or ten years ago it might have taken one or two weeks to produce a report but we are now in an environment where things have to happen far more quickly than that. And you have to venture outside your comfort zone and stretch yourself in a whole load of directions.

'I don't know anything about that' is just not a valid response any more. With the Internet you can do deep and rich research on most subjects and strike relationships with experts and commentators. Ignorance is not an option.

If you are prepared to venture into new areas you'll also find it a great platform for coming up with new ideas. Immersing yourself in a new area will be both daunting and stimulating, but it'll find you new ways of doing and thinking.

If your client is interested in opportunities in China, if the future of your business is in a new technology, there are no excuses. Your ability to learn and grow knows no boundaries other than TIME and INTENT.

OK, time is always a tough one, so just make sure you have the intent.

10
Get involved and get visible

If you're passionate about a new professional direction, don't hesitate to roll your sleeves up and get stuck in.

Katie has worked in HR for big companies in the City. She's taking a career break before embarking on a new direction; she wants to set up an art gallery. So she's got involved in a local art exhibition, helping out with marketing, sponsorship and organization. She's finding out everything about putting on an art show and gaining really valuable experience. It's a voluntary role, but by the end of the project she'll be an expert.

And a valuable lesson: *Go for it.*

Whatever 'it' is – your goal, ambition, aspiration, dream – start doing 'it' and, if you can, do it young. Whether student radio, school enterprise project, film extra – get involved and prove your talents.

While everyone else is hanging around the college common room or watching TV, you are actually taking that first early step on to the career ladder. And it's never too early to start.

When I started doing work experience at a radio station, I did everything I could. I presented a show, did the gig guide for another, did some technical operation on some shows, drove the outside broadcast vehicle (a lot of which I must admit I didn't do that well, especially the driving). But I was visible. So I got offered proper paid work by other producers and other shows. The presenter of the movie programme was away. Could I stand in for him? More opportunities flowed. Because I was doing so much I was perceived as that good safe pair of hands. I was visible and I was available.

Then, when I got to university I wanted to get some marketing experience, so I stood for and was elected as Publicity Officer for the student union. I sat on every student committee, I presented shows on the campus radio station, I DJ'd at the college disco – I was pretty visible. I admit that I had an ego, but you have to have an ego to succeed.

Just make sure everyone knows you for the right reasons, so be careful what you put about yourself on Facebook.

11

Don't listen to anyone who says 'no' to your ambition

Whatever your age or experience, if you have an idea, a goal or a dream – take the courage to *Leap!* regardless of what anyone else says.

It's fine to take advice from friends, family and mentors. Re-shape and shift your proposition if there's good reason to, use feedback to fine tune your ideas – but stick to your guns, don't let anyone persuade you not to do it at all. Ambition takes self-determination to succeed, so don't be swayed.

When I was in my final year at school I told my headmaster I wanted to study media at university and planned to pursue a career in broadcasting. Sitting in his office the headmaster suggested that was an impractical goal and brought out a pro-spectus on a course in company secretaryship and said, 'Here, you should do this course instead.'

To this day I have no idea why he did that, it seemed an odd piece of advice. But I ignored him anyway.

! Six months later I was presenting the gig guide on local radio.

! Twelve months later I was presenting a show on local radio.

! Ten years later I was asked to return to the school to advise students on careers in the media.

Part of me felt like not supporting the school that had failed to support my own ambition, but a bigger part of me realized the students probably needed all the help they could get.

My booth had the biggest queues.

12
Be real!

Be ambitious, yes. But be realistic.

I've met with people just starting out who talk of over-ambitious goals – turnover you know they cannot generate, crazy rates of growth, an over-inflated plan for acquisition and development. Knowing your limits is key. I have always taken an 'honest' approach to business: knowing when to say this project is too big for us, when to say we cannot deliver something. This pragmatism helps drive the business in the right direction and protects your risk.

Ambition and goal-setting are key to success but don't have false expectations about what is possible. Be realistic about what you can and can't do.

My own goals in life have always been realistic. Some quite simple: to be someone. To create something.

Others more specific: to work in radio; to work in TV; to work in the music industry; to recruit and manage my own team; to become an MD of a small business; to start my own business; to be a father; to write a book.

So set some targets of your own and make them realistic. For example:

! Who are your target clients?

! What are your target projects?

! What is your target turnover?

! What is your target profit?

Write down your goals and at the end of the year sit back and write down your achievements. Not just the obvious financial ones but also your achievements in personal development, the skills and experience you gained, the bits that counted for you.

Don't overcomplicate it, but goal-setting is an important way to set and track your achievements.

That's why they are called targets.

13
Follow your gut feeling

Go with your gut feeling.

You may want to consult others before embarking on a new strategy or direction, but always trust your instinct.

It's like when you ask a friend about a dilemma or decision, 'Should I?' or 'Shouldn't I?' when deep down, you *truly* know what to do before you even ask the question. Or when you have that moment of clarity on the tube or in the middle of the night. When you come up with that magic figure for your budget proposal. Getting the right answer is not always a science.

Instinct is such a valuable and underrated tool in the entrepreneur's toolkit. You don't need advisers and mentors for every decision. Because – and especially for the big ones – you'll know instinctively whether to take that risk on a project, invest in that new piece of software or take that managing director for lunch.

Just as you instinctively knew whether to take the *Leap!* in the first place. So, when you are struggling with decisions, remember your emotional response when you first had the dilemma. Nine times out of ten your final decision will reflect whatever you first felt, regardless of the analysis, evaluation and consulting you might have in between.

So why not save time – take a risk and trust your instinct. It's one of your most valuable tools, so use it.

14

Leverage what you've learnt

Before you *Leap!* from your proper job, remember to take all the lessons you have learnt with you. Exploit every bit of your experience.

Because your job working for someone else will help you when working for yourself. Years being an employee can help the 'How not to' as much as the 'How to'. So build up contacts and experiences. See what works, note what doesn't work. Use the workplace experience to learn all you can on budgeting, people management, project delivery, client care. You would probably be surprised by what you've learnt in your career.

People who have always worked for themselves are still capable of great success, but I would advocate a mixed bag of a few years' solid work experience before you take the *Leap!*. It's a great classroom and also a great reference point.

After all, if you never experienced first hand the tedium of working for someone else, how can you appreciate the freedom of working for yourself?

Working for someone else can limit your potential. You may be hungry to move on, to take on more responsibility but be denied the opportunity. When you go it alone, you're forever promoting yourself, stretching your skills in a whole load of directions, doing things you've always wanted to do, and also doing some things you never dreamed of doing.

15

Get out of the classroom

Some business success stories attribute their achievements to what they learnt at business school. I'm not a fan of business schools and MBAs because I don't believe you can learn much in a classroom; you can only really learn on the job. I was with two clients this morning. They are a two-person business. They debated about sending one of the partners on a training course but instead she jumped in at the deep end. She says she's learnt so much more actually doing the job than going on a training course and learning the theory.

Ten years ago I went on a management course, but there's little I can remember from it. What I have done in my job, on the other hand, is so memorable, what I did right and what I did wrong.

After all, the new business stars of today never went to business school. We've heard of the rap stars who learnt their business skills on the streets of New York, buying and selling to mates who have now extended their brands into record labels, clothing ranges, even vodka. One such rap star's business turnover was $90 million in year one.

No formal training. No grand plan. No rules. Just learning the basics and going for it.

So here's to the grass-roots entrepreneur, it's the best place to start. Never assume you have to go to business school or university to be successful.

You just need to have the right attitude.

16

Knock down the barriers

In a world of business with no rules, you have to cast your inhibitions aside and just get on with it. A friend of mine always wanted to be a writer. Not any kind of writing – she wanted to write erotica. But she had a serious job in finance and had never tried writing. Lots of people around her said, 'You can't be a writer because that's not what you do.' But who says? Why not?

So, she picked herself a pseudonym, got herself a hotmail address, and started writing and sending stories off to magazines and books. She told the magazines she was a writer. Not a wannabe writer, not an aspiring writer, but *a writer*. And editors liked her work. And they published her. Since she could hide behind the pseudonym, she had no inhibitions about claiming who or what she was and that gave her the confidence to do what she wanted. She said she was a writer and displayed such confidence that she got published.

Of course if she had written to them saying, 'I'm not a writer but have tried my hand at a few stories – would you have a look at them?' she would have got a very different response. A rejection, no doubt.

Break down the barriers, lose the inhibitions and you'll be more successful.

17

A focal point

As an adviser to start-ups and new businesses, I have never changed my mantra:

'Focus, Focus, Focus.'*

And I try to adhere to it myself. Namely:

! Focus on what you are good at.

! Focus on one area at a time.

! Focus on results.

! Focus on building revenues.

! Focus on building a profitable business.

Too many companies get too ambitious, too quick. Having ten great ideas is all well and good but you might need to put a few on the back burner to make sure you can concentrate on delivery of at least one. And you can rarely invoice for an idea alone; you usually invoice for the *delivery* of an idea.

---

* And you'll find 47 mentions of focus in this book (make that 48) as evidence.

So focus on your core competence and get a reputation for *one* thing. And stay focused on what you can do to directly contribute to your bottom line – how's that for motivation?

It's easy to get sidetracked, diverted to another area if you get bored with the first. But keep your eye on the goal and don't take it away until you've reached it.

18

Why failure's OK

I read an interview with a well-known entrepreneur the other day that said that the word 'failure' is not in his vocabulary.

But there's nothing wrong with a project or venture failing; I've had my fair share of failures. The experience it gives you in running a new project or venture will be really valuable.

An idea that gets fulfilled but ultimately fails is better than an idea that stays in a notepad or on a to-do list.

Sometimes you'll have bad news on a pitch or a deal will fall flat and you have to keep optimistic, salvage something positive from a heap of mess.

Stand back from it, count to ten.

I lost a pitch but went back to the client with an upbeat message, saying I was sorry not to have won it but that I still had some ideas to contribute. He thanked me for my positive reaction to bad news and asked me to stay in touch, with the potential for more work later.

Another time I had a problem with some suppliers who'd let me down. I picked the phone up straight away and let them know I was pissed off. And then I counted to ten. Or a hundred and ten more like. I explained in a dispassionate way what they had done wrong. The result? They apologized and did their utmost to keep me happy.

The problems caused me a lot of (unnecessary) grief, but by staying calm and standing back, it didn't get out of hand.

So try to be constructive when projects or relationships fail, because you can build better business as a result.

And if you mess up on a project or with a client, that's fine. Say so.

'I f***ed up.'

And move on.

19

You'd better believe it ...

When I started out in management I bored colleagues by saying, 'I could have managed a biscuit factory.' I never did get involved in biscuit production but it was a belief I have always held that I can be successful at most things and my management and business skills are transferable across a range of industries.

You may think that sounds like arrogance but it's actually self-belief. Believing in your own abilities is a powerful force and you've got to have that belief, that self-confidence, otherwise you'll really struggle. Launching a new business and then questioning your abilities to progress it can be a very destructive cycle. You *have* to believe it has success potential.

An ex-client of mine is a successful counsellor. But he's only done that for two years. His background is in property and retail. I asked him why he became a counsellor. One reason was to prove to himself that he could do anything he wanted and he's proved it to be true; he can turn his hand to most things. And some people are good at that; others are only good in their single sphere of expertise – take them out of their comfort zone and they'll sink.

The Icelandic entrepreneur Magnus Scheving started out as a builder and carpenter and was a motivational speaker at the weekends (how's that for a combination?). When he was in his early 20s he made a bet with a friend that anyone could succeed at anything they wanted; his friend bet him to master aerobics and he became an aerobics champion. He then went on to bring all that experience together to launch a children's TV show, book and musical. There is a man with self-belief. If you get enough people to have faith in a goal, it will happen.

When you are developing a project or an idea, you have to believe it will happen. If you don't, you risk it not coming off. Visualizing that end goal, seeing how the end product will be consumed is a powerful force in thinking positively.

Self-doubt, on the other hand, will not deliver success. Let's face it, you will have days when your confidence is not at its best – but a confident and positive outlook will breed success.

Just be sure to manage your own expectations. I was pitching for a big assignment and decided to take a very positive approach to the process; I was extremely confident that I would get the project. So much so that, as I was waiting in the client's reception *before* I went in to the meeting, I scribbled on my notepad, 'I've got it'. As a result, I came across very well in the client meeting and they liked my confident and positive approach.

Unfortunately they saw someone even better than me later that week and he got the gig. I didn't win the project. It was a big blow.

So self-belief is important; always have a confident and positive approach, but if you big yourself up to win a project, just remember it's a long way to fall if you don't pull it off.

20

From city trader to sole trader

I am sitting in a café in the heart of the 'City', London's financial centre where rules abound in both business and working practices. Parameters to what you do and how you do it. Although it has changed there are still rules as to what you wear, of what hours you work, of what your status is. This is anathema to the *scrambled up world of work*; it's a world of conforming to expectations, of doing the predictable.

When I started working in television in the late 1980s, I used to catch the train with old school friends who were on their way to their jobs in the City. 'Not working today?' they'd ask. Because they didn't get it – in their world a guy going somewhere in jeans could not have been going to work. And – thank goodness – most of that has changed.

In the City, in banks and financial institutions, there is undoubtedly a lot of talent. Workers are supplying their intellectual capital to employers, but strip away the corporate layers and how enterprising are the constituent parts? Or are their talents about being part of a team with a corporate infrastructure; is their power about being part of that critical mass?

Stick them in Prêt A Manger with a phone and a laptop and how would they fare, not as city traders but as sole traders? Who would thrive and who would struggle?

Because taking the *Leap!* is all about uncovering the entrepreneur within. And some will find that easier than others:

> 'Some people will find it a challenge to leave an established work environment where they have busy colleagues and a support infrastructure around them, and walk into a quiet, empty, serviced office somewhere with nothing but a phone, a laptop, a desk and a bunch of good ideas. You have to start building something from scratch; moving from the buy side to the sell side is a shock for many people and it can be very lonely at the start. Equally you might have the best business plan in the world but you still have to have that passion, energy and desire to make it work.'

Adam Bennett, co-founder of Hatstand who quit the City for life as an entrepreneur.

21

Conformity sucks

A good friend of mine got stuck in a rut at her old company. She worked in a culture where she was convinced that loyalty and success was measured by wearing a suit, turning up to work early, not taking a lunch break, leaving late. That was what her boss did and if you wanted to conform, that's what you had to do. She worked in an oppressive office environment, with poor natural light and desks crammed into too small a space. She didn't even like wearing a suit.

In her job, accountability and measuring performance weren't about productivity or how many ideas you had; it was about being heard and seen, the perception being that if you arrived early and left late then you must have been doing something right.

The day she walked away from that job, she felt liberated. She had no idea what she was going to do next but she felt she could start listening to her heart. You've got to feel comfortable in your skin, confident that your work reflects at least some of your personality. If not, change it. If you don't like wearing a suit to work, don't wear one. If your employer doesn't like it, maybe it's time to change your employer. What's the point of compromising who you are? Why conform for the sake of it?

Say bollocks to conformity. Listen to your heart, shed the shackles of corporate life and take a liberating *Leap!* away to the *scrambled up world*.

22

Why catalysts count

Unless you have some grand plan from an early age – that you were always going to start a business – inevitably there's going to be a catalyst for taking the *Leap!*. Maybe you are sick of your current job, unhappy in your life, stuck in a rut? You may be fed up working hard for someone else for minimal reward and feel you can achieve more on your own.

Certainly more and more people are taking the *Leap!* and a big driver is dissatisfaction:

! Dissatisfaction with working for someone else, where you have to abide by rules you don't like.

! Dissatisfaction when you hit a glass ceiling and feel your ambition is limited by your employer.

! Dissatisfaction with the opportunities in the job market being too limited and inflexible.

! Dissatisfaction with the status quo and a feeling that you just want to do something different.

! Dissatisfaction with the fact that you can't dictate new working practices when you become a parent.

Or you may have some 'lifestyle' reasons:

! You're unhappy in life and want or need a change.

! Your job is making you stressed or you're feeling ill.

! You want to restore a better work/life balance.

! You have become a parent.

! You just want to be in control.

! You don't want to spend hours a day commuting to your workplace.

Sometimes you might be forced to take the *Leap!*. Redundancy can be a catalyst for trying new career routes with the safety net of your redundancy pay to support you trying new things. Redundancy may force you to think, 'What do I do next?' And, of course, you may not have an answer, but you have to do *something*, and you don't have much time to make a decision. So redundancy can be your biggest break.

Or, you may have more of a proactive reason: you have this fantastic idea, a goal or a yearning to build a new business, something you've been aching to do for years or just an idea you had on the tube. Some take the *Leap!* in their 30s or 40s when they have become disillusioned with their jobs; others when they are younger because it is much lower-risk quitting your job when you don't have all that financial responsibility like kids and mortgages to worry about.

Me? I had a mix of motives:

! Ultimately the job was making me unhappy. I was over-stressed with too much on my plate. I'd become a victim of my own success: I was given new projects and ventures to run but only if I retained the old ones where I'd been success-ful. The company didn't want to risk losing my strengths in one area for me to try a new one.

! Plus, I was doing the double-whammy: working too hard and playing too hard – I was going to burn myself out. I felt un-well.

! I knew I needed a change.

Catalysts are important. If I hadn't got stressed, felt ill or got fed up then I would never have pressed the pause button and stood back. If I had just fast-forwarded through corporate life, I might never have made the change (hey, I might still be in my old job now ...).

At the time I could not rationalize or articulate it so clearly. It was more urgent than that. It was that I needed to do *something*. I needed to make a *change*. And *quick*. And that conviction is all you need to take the *Leap!*

You might just have an inkling or a feeling. That's all it takes. So once you've worked out you want to change, don't hang around too long to *Leap!*. Because it'll make you an unhappy and un-productive worker. The sooner you liberate yourself, the sooner you can release all that positive energy and start afresh.

23
It's a risky business

Why don't people *Leap*?

Three reasons:

1   Risk,

2   Risk, and

3   Risk.

Ask anyone what's stopping them taking the *Leap!* and, apart from a lack of self-belief, not wanting to take the risk is the reason most people give. They have kids, they have mortgages and they are frightened of losing financial stability.

And they are right about that – this is risky business. Ask yourself this:

What's the worst thing that can happen? It all fails and you have to go back and get a proper job. But at least you *tried*.

If you've been in your proper job for a long time, your resistance to change will be greater. You may have become institutionalized to the culture of your old organization, and the idea of leaving not just your job, but your office and all that represents may be extremely frightening.

Because an office is more than a business; it's a culture and a rich network of social and professional relationships; of support and dependency – it's a safety net. If you strip those layers away it can be scary.

People also stay in jobs longer if they like their co-workers. That may seem an odd reason not to take the *Leap!* but if your colleagues are like family, breaking up that social unit is not going to be a priority.

If you're risk averse then this isn't for you. But accept from the outset that there will be highs and lows. You have to be a glass half-full kind of person, because a half-empty approach will get you nowhere.

In the old economy you were a cog, neatly segmented into a role in an organizational structure. Now it's different – you can survive without all that structure and comfort, and achieve so much more. *If* you are prepared to take a risk.

But, of course, it might get uncomfortable.

24

'Easy'??!

For one naïve moment in 2000 I thought business would be easier now I had taken the *Leap!* I thought it would be 'easier' not having a proper job, without any boss or board to answer to.

I started to earn more money, work fewer days and enjoy less responsibility. But that was just the beginning.

Beyond that first year it was anything but easy. It was very hard work. Much tougher than a proper job where you have a guarantee of a pay packet at the end of the month. It was not a case of taking the easy way out, rather the hard way out.

I met a former colleague the other day and told him I was writing a book about quitting 'the 9–5'. 'But you haven't *quit* the 9–5,' he said, 'you've gone 24/7.' And he's right. It's not about quitting corporate life for something easier; it's about a new way of working. And in the *scrambled up world of work* there are zero guarantees of success.

So I offer you three words:

   Go for it.

Oh, and three more:

   And good luck.

25
Go for it ...

If you want to do something new, to take that *Leap!* from the confines of your corporate life to start afresh, to relocate, or to follow your dreams; if you have even a 35% inkling that you should do it, then *do it*. Because you're unlikely to ever get a 100% affirmation.

So take your *Leap!* and set up that property company, yoga centre, management consultancy.

Everything involves risk.

You'll always find reasons *not* to do it. The longer you leave it, the greater the chance that you'll get stuck in a rut and never have the courage to *Leap!*

I know people who have stayed in jobs ten years and always *meant* to leave. And they're still unhappy, still dreaming of 'what if?' and wondering what life is like on the other side, wishing they'd gone for it.

Sometimes you need a catalyst or that defining moment when you say 'bollocks to the status quo' and you take that *Leap!* into the unknown.

So say it now.

Part Two
ENTERPRISE

Once you have decided to *Leap!* there's a whole load of realities to consider.

How you define yourself, how you find clients, what you charge clients, how you juggle everything from admin to sales in order to be successful.

And the bottom line is: there has to be a bottom line.

So you've got to be enterprising in everything you do.

And let's start with the basics.

1

The bare basics

When you're getting started, you need to consider the essence of your new life.

Life in the *scrambled up world* is always unpredictable, sometimes scary, almost always liberating. And whatever changes you'll have to make, whatever the highs and lows, the bare facts remain the same:

All I have is my bare hands, a bunch of contacts and a few ideas. And with that I have to make a whole load of money.

It's that simple.

Gulp. And that scary.

There's no pay cheque going in your account any more. There are no guarantees.

This is going to be different.

2

Having the idea

Sometimes you'll spend a whole day, a whole week, or even longer … searching for an idea, for the clarity of vision or a strategy, brainstorming that killer business idea, that answer to your problems. But you'll get nowhere; you'll get frustrated but you'll still sit manacled to your desk, laptop or notepad and get nowhere.

But all it takes is one single, simple, short moment of clarity to get *it*.

Not always a eureka/light bulb moment, not always *that big* a sense of idea, but you'll get it. That solution, strategy, winning product or perfect marketing idea. Something, anything that will make a significant difference to your business or to your future.

This may sound cheesy but this is what it feels like to me. Your eyes scanning the screen, a page or a vista, eyes searching across a landscape and not seeing anything. And then suddenly … like a silver lining to a cloud, a glimpse of late sunlight on a cloud-filled afternoon, you get that return-on-investment, *the* moment of clarity – and you'll smile as it all becomes clear and you have it.

Not even a minute, just a second of that recognition that it's a good idea is enough.

And when you see that vision, when you articulate it, it's a climax.

And that's what enterprise is all about.

3
Do it yourself

When you work for yourself, you'll probably have a portfolio of business commitments and roles rather than a single discipline or activity. Because there's winning the business, doing the business, billing for the business, handling client relations – and that's just the start.

The notion of portfolio working is a good one – for the self-employed it helps validate what we do and how we do it. Most of us do a mix of 'stuff' in our working week: sitting at a screen, meeting clients and suppliers, managing production, writing documents, phoning .clients, crafting proposals and pitches. Similarly, you may have elected to have a variety of stuff you do:

1   Things you do because you have to (the stuff that pays the bills).

2   Things you do because you like to.

3   Things you do because you are good at them.

That's a portfolio.

For a one-person business you'll be CEO, sales director, secretary, IT department and accounts department all in one job description. You may be your own boss but you're also the office junior. And that means you have to win the business *and* do the photocopying.

This is going to stretch you in all kinds of directions. It will get confusing and if you're a one-person company no one's going to congratulate you when you have won a new piece of business.

So you're going to have to add 'patting yourself on the back' to your multi-tasking to-do list.

4

Making something (anything) out of nothing

For most of us, all we have is our intellectual capital – that's the raw material given to us all. And with that we have to create *something* (a product, project, event, service, a great business) from *nothing* (a blank notepad, an empty spreadsheet, a blank document on your screen or a bare order book).

If you are self-employed and also work at home, friends in 'proper jobs' may tease you and suggest you might watch daytime TV or get up late every day now you work for yourself. That's because that's what they think they might do if they worked from home since they only have a comprehension of what it's like on someone else's time and at someone's else's expense.

But this is different.

In the *scrambled up world of work*, self-accountability is where it's at. If you do choose to get up late and watch TV in the afternoon then how are you going to get paid? That's the crux – you have to pose this critical question:

'What can I do today to add value to another human being's life which means at the end of the month I can send them an invoice?'

And that is the essence of running a business.

And it's a question I struggle with constantly. Because lots of clients will like you and many people will like your ideas but getting someone to *pay you* for them, well that is a different and more difficult matter.

How do you get someone to pay you? By providing something they need, something they want from you, and can't get anywhere else at that price, at that quality, with that experience.

But there's a catch:

They need to have a budget.

And that might sound a bit bloody obvious but 'haven't got a budget' is something you'll hear time and time again from all your clients. Often I will win business but I am told 'we haven't got a budget, so we'll have to find one', which means they haven't got much money. Sometimes you'll have a client who says from the outset, 'This is our budget'. Much better.

But clients are demanding, and after all it's their prerogative – they're paying you.

But you'll still get clients who want something for nothing. Clients who want lots upfront, for nothing. Clients who want the product but will only pay 50% of the asking price. These kind of clients are very common.

Clients who want it now, who have the full budget, and who are easy to deal with – these are rare.

So when you find your dream clients, *whatever you do* look after them properly and never take them for granted.

Because you need them. Big time.

5

Wrapping up your know-how

Your 'intellectual capital' is at the heart of what you trade. That's what you are providing in the marketplace:

! knowledge,

! information,

! expertise,

! talent,

! ideas,

! a product.

So you need to identify and define carefully what your product is. What's your offering? What makes it compelling and memorable? Why will people pay to get it?

Ask yourself, if information is power, how do I leverage what I know – my know-how, market knowledge and intelligence – for commercial benefit? How do I wrap it up into a saleable package? And that is the crux of it.

My current business sells marketing ideas and consultancy services. Sometimes it's tough because successful clients don't think they need marketing and under-performing clients say they can't afford marketing. So you have to position it differently; offer them something they need, or give them a great idea. Because business always needs great ideas to succeed. So I wrap up my offering as ideas-based, providing solutions to clients' problems and challenges.

Our ideas are simple yet effective; because we have a fresh perspective. An outsider taking a fresh look at an old problem. And never underestimate the power – and the value – of that distance and insight.

I went to a meeting and the prospective client was really impressed with my ideas that had been a breath of fresh air to him. Hey, I said at the close of the meeting, all I have is a bunch of ideas. They may or may not work, but that's all I have to bring to the venture.

Which is great because that is exactly what he needed: an injection of fresh ideas and I was his fix.

Dead easy for me, dead effective for him.

It may come easy for you but your clients have probably been racking their collective brains for months on this one. And that means they should appreciate the value of your input or service. Just remember that when you work out what to charge them.

My partner runs an online business selling vinyl stickers for interiors. But she doesn't focus the sell on stickers themselves; rather, she sells wall designs. The stickers themselves may have little value but the *idea* of what to do with them, how to cost-effectively enhance a room, how to brighten up a living space – that gives the proposition value.

And giving the customer value means you can charge more money for a product.

Well, you can try anyway.

6

'Sell' is not an expletive

When I started work in my early 20s, I didn't 'do' sales. I didn't think it was something I needed to be bothered with. How naive I was. When I got more responsibility and moved up the ranks, of course I saw that the essence of every single business is sales. No exception.

Sell is not a dirty word; it's what we all do and you'll need to embrace it to be successful.

Too many think that being a good salesperson is about wearing a smart suit and hawking a PowerPoint presentation round to visit targets. Or worse, cold-calling companies trying to get them interested in your product or service. It's not. You're actually selling yourself, your ideas, your product and your abilities.

Being a good salesperson is about being flexible in your approach; identifying and recognizing what currency of communication will turn on your target clients; and communicating that effectively. It's hard work, rarely easy. Some of us are better at it than others, but we all have to sell. Staring at a blank spreadsheet with no orders can be daunting but remember, sales is about establishing relationships. If you are going to be an entrepreneur, you are going to be selling all the time.

Don't jump in with a hard sell; learn to understand your target's culture, objectives, challenges and needs. It takes time, patience – and often a lunch or two – but once you get to know your client it's easy to understand what it will take for them to make that commitment to your ideas and your product.

People talk about the trick of *closing* a sale as one of the most difficult things in business. Well, don't underestimate *opening* a sale, just starting the sales process. Undoubtedly this is one of the toughest things when you work for yourself.

Of course sometimes a client will approach you or respond to a piece of marketing which makes it an easier sell. The psychology of them wanting something from you will aid your ability to strike a good deal. But doing that deal, negotiating at the right price still takes skill and experience.

So put on your sales hat. Getting knock-backs and rejections is never fun, but winning a bit of business – now that always feels good.

7

Expressing yourself

When I started out I was just 'Ian Sanders' trading as myself. I didn't have a separate brand name, I didn't have a company or a job title. I was just 'Ian Sanders' – that was my offering. I felt quite 'naked', but also it was quite refreshing: all I had to offer was me. It was black and white. Hire me or don't hire me. Do you want me or not?

When it comes to what you call yourself, consider the benefits of a brand name over your own name. A brand name breaks the limitations and perceptions of a sole trader brand. It will enable more opportunities because a third party brand will punch above its weight and open doors. Clients may get nervous about trusting their business to one person; a brand offers them comfort and reassurance.

But a brand can also mislead; it can tell a different story. So don't use a brand to bullshit. If you work out of the spare room don't call the company 'The Global Corporation' and don't call yourself the CEO on the business cards. Especially if you're a sole trader.

Think carefully. The brand name on the website, on your business card, in an ad, will say so much about you.

Similarly, other ways of defining yourself are just as important. When I started out as a consultant, 'consultancy' was a dirty word because for many clients it has connotations of overpaid and under-efficient management consultants. So I had to find other ways of describing myself: project manager, adviser.

Be sure to find your right currency of definition. It's like your label. What does it say?

8

Learn to juggle ... well

A constant theme once you have taken the *Leap!* is juggling: juggling disciplines, projects and tasks. Sometimes the workplace can prepare you for this but if you were institutionalized in a single-discipline department all your working life, then it's going to come as a shock.

In my one of my staff roles, I was tasked with producing a big event. It was all-consuming getting focused on a specific goal and all the deliverables that were needed, spending time on-site, travelling, meeting suppliers and crew. But my boss, the CEO, said I also had to manage a small department in a completely different discipline at the same time. I was incredulous: 'But they are *completely* different projects; there's no way I can manage them at the same time,' I complained. The CEO replied that was what business was like. And he was right (but he also got someone to do two jobs for the price of one). Which is probably why he was the CEO.

Whether I agreed with him or not it was a great learning experience, it was hard work but it taught me a good lesson in juggling.

In the *scrambled up world of work* you'll have to juggle lots of projects; small annoying ones with big stimulating ones. There's no option to let anything slip.

When you have a proper job, you may have 27 things to do at the same time but you probably have a single focus – in your role you are focused on a corporate goal, building revenues, developing a new product or whatever: it's homogeneous.

But once you start your own business you don't pick and choose workload. You won't always go from assignment A to assignment B, from client A to client B. More likely, it will all happen at *the same time*; each project will overlap or coincide like a network of Venn diagrams. So at any given time you could be working on multiple projects for multiple clients. And you'll be expected to live and breathe each one simultaneously, each with its own unique set of goals and challenges. It is not homogeneous.

Managing that plurality is different to anything you ever did in the workplace, there are no valid excuses for why you neglected one project in favour of another. So switch your brain and think plural.

Yes it's hard. When you're living and breathing one project, you have to field calls on another, troubleshoot a problem on a third, all at the same time as trying to drum up new business.

And that means you have to try not to drop any of the balls.

Some don't or can't pull it off. I know some self-employed workers who can't deal with that: their head is down on one project and they ignore problems on another. Worse still, they ignore communications because they just can't keep all the balls in the air.

9
Turning a contact into a client

You know lots of people. You have loads of numbers stored in your mobile phone, have a stack of email addresses on your computer, have a list of Christmas cards you send.

You are unlikely to be short of contacts but, admittedly, you may be short of clients.

So you need to perform some magic: you need to turn a contact into a client:

1   Identify a contact that you think might make a good client. What makes a good client? Someone who you can sell something to; someone who wants what you can give him or her; but, more crucially, someone who has a budget. Because without a budget you can forget sending an invoice. And without an invoice you don't have a business.

2   That contact is now a target. Build a relationship with your target: get close to them, get to know them even better.

3   Identify a need. What is their 'hot button'? Do they need to enter a new market? What is their objective this week? What will impress their boss or board or help them be a success? Or do they just need to grow sales?

4   Leverage your knowledge to provide a solution to their need. To fulfil that need in a *unique* way that they can't get anywhere else in terms of: the idea; the price; what makes it different; and the fact that you can introduce them to one of your other contacts or provide that value-added service.

5   Sell that solution to your target. Lobby, persuade and encourage them to work with you. Create a compelling offer and provide the best service you can.

You have to work at it. Being passive is not an option. You have to be proactive in nurturing relationships and contacts, otherwise they'll die.

This isn't as easy as it may sound and once you've satisfied 1–4, the final sell is sometimes the most difficult – getting commitment.

Securing commitment and winning business doesn't always rely on giving the best presentation. More often it's about chemistry – how did you get on with your target client?

Clients will use you because they like you and trust that you will look after their interests, their project and their brand. You won't necessarily be best friends, but you need to focus on getting the relationship right.

And increasingly it's less about a formal us–them pitch. It's about communication, an exchange of ideas, a meeting; it's about how you get on, and the difference your contribution could make.

So recognize the importance of establishing, retaining and managing relationships.

10

Charge them!

As management writer Charles Handy noted in his commentary on the changing role of the individual in business (2001, *The Elephant and the Flea*, Hutchinson), more and more people are aware that their knowledge has a marketable value. They are reluctant to sell knowledge for what Handy calls 'a time-based contract', i.e. a wage; they would rather be more enterprising and charge a fee or a royalty for their input.

This is an important lesson if you are starting out in business because your value should not be related to how long it took you to produce a project or a piece of work (nor indeed what the costs of production were). It's about the value of that contribution to the client. Handy observes that, in a staff job, you sell your talents in exchange for a salary package but, unless you have shares or share options, your gain is limited and not related to the success of your ideas. You gave up rights to those ideas as an individual and handed them to the corporation.

In the *scrambled up world of work*, independents retain control of knowledge and their ideas and charge fees accordingly.

Setting your prices at the right level is difficult, but critical. Charge your products and services too low and you risk jeopardizing your business viability. Charge them too high and you'll get a reputation for being too expensive and you could lose business potential.

Do make sure you charge enough; don't undervalue your services because pricing is the difference between break-even and a decent profit, between failure and success.

If you get your rates wrong and you need to change them, that's fine. But remember, it's often easier to reduce your prices than put them up.

Sometimes (i.e. mostly) it's hard making money and sometimes (i.e. rarely) it's easy. Your approach to charging will make all the difference.

A traditional way of pricing was to look at the direct costs of production or delivery and add a crude percentage as the profit margin. That approach fails to reflect the worth of the product or service. So you have to start the other way round: what is the end-product worth in the marketplace? What value do clients see in it? What would they be prepared to pay?

A bloody difficult question, but that's what you have to work out. And while you're pondering that one, the next question is – can the client afford it? Because you don't want to price your product too high for a client that might not be able to afford it, especially if you are starting out when *some revenues* are certainly better than *no revenues*.

11

Make sure you are valued

Unless you are selling a commoditized offering – web hosting, units of equipment – you probably won't have set prices for what you are selling, so you shouldn't try to oversimplify what services cost. It will vary from project to project, from client to client, market to market.

The value of ideas to a client is huge. It may have taken only 60 seconds to think of something, but the simplest ideas are often the most successful, and that should come at a price.

Some clients might not understand the worth of your service. Some of my clients have changed the brief on a project or asked for add-ons and been surprised when I have explained that extras cost extra. And whilst it's fine and good practice to throw in extras for free, similarly clients need to appreciate and value the service being provided. I stopped working with a client because they didn't get it. They didn't like it that every time they asked for new deliverables, they would cost more (although sometimes I did give them for free). But that was an important principle for me: business is commercial and if they value their brand, they need to make the right investment. When I said we needed to charge more for doing more, we parted company, because they didn't work like that.

And that was a price I had to pay for our principles – I lost a client but I didn't want to concede what I saw as commercial business practice in order to keep them.

Never undervalue what you do. Think carefully about how you position your value in the marketplace.

It's a bit like the question, 'What's better – a cheap, crap holiday or an expensive, good one?'

Think about it.

12

Doing the deal

Once you've set your price and you're convincing a client you're worth it, you'll start a negotiation.

And you'll do a lot of negotiation. You'll agree to do a project for a small fee because the client is new and you want to show flexibility/willing and, besides, they said it was a simple one. But then every time you do that, you end up over-delivering, and the project is never that simple. So you learn a lesson, to charge more the next time.

But it's difficult charging more 'next time'. Where you are managing a job and have suppliers to pay, you will try to put a decent margin on for the important project management element but, inevitably, where you have to reduce costs, yours is the wedge that gets squeezed. And you end up sweating for not a lot.

So you need to be good at negotiating. Sometimes it's not about carefully budgeting out a project line by line, it's about an intuition of how much the client values the project or what they want to pay. It's about anticipating their expectations.

But you need to have a well-prepared budget, because as soon as you get into negotiation that's when you need the ammunition about your real costs in delivering the product or service. If you can be transparent with clients about your cost breakdown, you might have a better negotiation. Show them how they are getting value for money. Show them why they should do the deal with you.

Ask what is the obstacle to the other party doing a deal with you. Then take that obstacle away. If it's price, say to the client, 'If I can get the price down do we have a deal?' If the client agrees – and if you can get the price down – they have no excuses as to not concluding a deal with you. Or ask the other party what it would take to conclude a deal. Deliver what they need.

Whatever way you do deals, you'll have to be flexible. Different 'sweeteners' (money off, big lunches, added extras) will swing different clients. Find their currency, talk their language and do the deal.

13

Enterprise is the only way

In this new world of work, business is rarely black and white.

Much of business is about commodities: we supply a distinct service or a product to a client and we get paid in return. But it's not always that simple.

Friends of mine who work in traditional jobs don't understand the notion that sometimes as much as 70% of my working week is not directly about revenue generation. There'll be whole days of research, writing, administration, invoicing, biz dev, project and idea development, and meeting new people that are about the maintenance and development of my business. And I can't send an invoice to anyone for any of it.

Similarly, some relationships with clients can take a long while to come to fruition. Going from meeting #1 to invoice #1 can take forever. To succeed you'll need a whole stack of patience, vision and courage. Oh yeah, and optimism. And not forgetting deep pockets. Some clients may require your investment in their being entertained before you win their business, and there are no guarantees it'll even come off.

Other times you may work on a project with a less than tangible return and it's tough quantifying your value, measuring your impact. The challenge is: how can I monetize my contribution, my idea? And this is just part of life once you've made the *Leap!*. Because you have to be flexible, open-minded and receptive to different ways of doing business, but you also have to stay focused on how you can make money.

What I do is very simple: I shut myself away in a room and find enterprising ways to 'earn a living'.

And there is no other option than to be enterprising.

14

Why being a chameleon can be a good thing

Sometimes it's good to be a chameleon. When you have a broad portfolio you are different things to different people:

! A writer to an editor.

! A marketing specialist to that MD.

! A head of design studio to that marketing exec.

! A web aficionado to that sales director.

So you've got to cherry pick from a number of styles and approaches so you can talk the respective different languages of the clients.

The onus is on *you* to be flexible, not the other way round.

Some clients will know you for certain skills, others for different ones. I was introduced to a contact last week as a 'radio expert'. I'm not an expert within the radio industry but, having worked in and around radio for ten years plus, I know radio and outside the industry have value as an 'expert'. So don't be quick to pigeonhole yourself with a single professional identity; it's more enterprising to be a chameleon.

So bring your phrase book, and be ready to speak a different language.

15
A toe in the water

Taking the *Leap!* is always about taking a risk but you can also minimize risk by trying out ventures while you are still in the comfort of your old job. I know a guy who has his day job but also runs an online business selling batteries for MP3 players. It doesn't take him much time, it doesn't generate big revenues and, who knows, one day he may ditch the job and do batteries full time, but in the meantime he's just trying it out. You can set up an Internet trading operation for next to nothing – it's a no-brainer. The only risk is your upfront cost of production.

A woman I know has a successful day job working full time as a designer, but also does freelance design jobs in her spare time. She's pulled off a great result: all the fun of a mixed portfolio but with the stability of a salary. You can also start small and test your entrepreneurial abilities doing some eBay or Amazon marketplace trading in your spare time, seeing how much money you can make reselling goods. If you get the buzz and you're good at it, that's a good sign. And if you don't get the buzz, that's also a sign.

If you have a portfolio of interests and you want to look at a new venture, remember you don't need to ditch everything else. You can do it alongside your existing projects.

I was introduced to someone who wanted to set up a new venture. I am working with her in a low-risk way, having a basic presence online and running the operation complementary to my other interests. Sure, it may become my core activity someday but it's a great way of spreading your entrepreneurial spirit. It's not a question of establishing a 'proper' start-up with funding requirements for staff and premises; it's not as if we have quit our 'proper' jobs and have a massive pressure for the new venture to work; it's a great way of having some variety in our portfolios.

So don't be shy of doing more than one thing.

Just so long as you remain focused about the requirements of each venture; you have to reconcile that with your time and resources – you don't want to spread yourself too thin.

16

Funding ain't often fun

Some new business ideas need stacks of money; others need small amounts to get going. But one way or another, most need some kind of funding just to get started, from small stuff like office furniture at Ikea to bigger stuff like product stock or taking a stand at that trade show.

So you'll need funding. A financial safety net of some description is great if you have personal savings to dip into as your start-up budget. Otherwise you'll need to generate funding from a third party.

'Getting funding from third parties' is a bit of an anachronism because it ain't fun and it won't involve throwing many parties.

Unless you're lucky.

Lucky in meeting a wealthy investor who is happy to hand over some funds but happy to stay hands-off; lucky because your husband's family has stacks of cash; or lucky because your business idea is so damn good you have a queue of investment angels lining up to offer you deals. (*Them* lining up to see *you*? They must be angels …)

Getting third-party funding is not only hard but also gives someone else an influence on how you run your business. Subsequently you may end up feeling constrained rather than liberated. Funding from an investor may only represent a 20% share in your business, but that's another voice to listen to. He or she may only have a 20% say in what you do, but they'll have a 100% interest in their stake. And you can bet they'll be calling the shots, or trying to.

So you have to weigh up the value of those funds versus having to listen to someone else. Because at worst that could mean diluting your business objectives – or even doing something you don't want to do – to keep them happy.

It might be easier just to talk to your bank manager and try friends and family. That way you can stay in control of the business and you don't have to dilute your ownership. And if you do need to consider serious fund raising, get an expert involved to help you.

So keep it simple, keep your borrowing needs lean, and don't stretch yourself when it comes to the skills required for serious fund raising.

17

The power of collaboration

If you team up with other like-minded people you can strengthen your own offering. Consider the power – and perception – of a team of five people working for themselves versus a team of just one.

Which was a lesson I learnt. I was a one-man business but had always brought freelance talent in to facilitate projects. The perception was that I was too small – it was just me. So I formed an umbrella venture with my contacts, marketing not just me but my copywriter, designers and web developer as part of a single offering. The market perception of a bigger offering meant we could win more projects. Clients may feel concerned about putting important projects with a one-person business unit; they feel more comfortable if there is the perception of back-up and a bigger team. In reality the team was virtual, still run by me pulling in who was needed when; but my clients saw strength in numbers.

Just make sure your collaboration is focused and in your best interests. Over the past seven years I've been approached by so many self-employed friends and contacts suggesting collaboration. But you have to answer 'for what purpose?' Don't dilute your potential for success by unfocused collaboration that doesn't add to your portfolio and/or doesn't pay. Stay focused on a goal whenever you team up with others.

If you have a good rationale that can reinvigorate and strengthen your offering, not only does it give you a bunch of co-workers to keep you company, but it also means you have more ways of making money. Because you are selling not just yourself, not just your new team, but also the critical mass of your combined offering. And that critical mass gives you the potential to be a bigger player.

And how's that for enterprise?

18

Introduction time

One of your most valuable sales tools is word of mouth. So communicating exactly what you do to your contacts is really useful because that's your strongest route to getting business.

My financial adviser happened to share an office with the chairman of a major music industry company. When I needed some advice on a music venture I was involved with he set up a lunch with this guy, whose advice was invaluable. He would never have seen me otherwise. We got on well and he then invited me to a party where I was able to fast-track the development of my contacts in that sector. He also paid for lunch – nice guy.

So take an enterprising approach to whom you work with. Appoint suppliers and service providers on the basis of how useful it may be for your business. Hire that PR company not just because they are good but also because they might introduce some of their clients to you.

Your black book is valuable not just for getting your own clients, but also when it comes to making recommendations or introductions. I am often asked by clients, friends and associates to recommend a supplier or collaborator. I like being a 'connector' and I get satisfaction when the jigsaw of contacts comes together. You introduce your contacts to each other, they get on well and find synergies in their ambitions and philosophies, and go off and work together. It's like when a dinner party goes well. You can't always monetize these relationships/introductions but I find it very satisfying.

I introduced a radio presenter to his agent; now they are living together with a baby.

And that is one introduction I cannot send an invoice for.

19
Know how to make money

I took a client to lunch the other day.

'We'd better talk business, otherwise you can't claim it on expenses!' he joked.

'Claim as expenses'?

What the client seemed to forget, regardless of what we talked about, is that it's my money and it's coming out of my pocket. Whether you run your own small business or work for a huge one, try acting like it's your money. You'll have a different way of looking at things.

And your approach to money will influence your success; if you are the kind of person who is good with your own finances, then you're going to be more effective in business. If you're the kind of person who never knows how much is in your own bank account and forgets to pay your bills, however damn creative you are, you may suffer from not having the right approach.

In order to be successful you're going to have to take a view on how much money you can make on something. You don't *have* to be hard-nosed to run a successful company but you do need to be savvy.

Financial prudence is essential. Because running a successful business is very simple. At the heart of good financial management, it's about keeping revenues up and keeping costs down. So there's no need to over-complicate it.

20

Counting your money

Make sure you know what you're earning and what you're spending. That may sound so obvious but you'll need 'checks and balances' in place to make sure in a snapshot – at this very moment – you know your financial health. Because that is one of your key indicators to success. It may sound a bit tedious but it's crucial to be organized when it comes to money. So make sure you can answer questions like:

! What's your projected profit this month?

! What's your current biggest client in terms of profit?

! What's your most profitable project?

You need these at your fingertips. And to answer these you are going to need to have reliable mechanisms for recording expenses and revenue, whether a spreadsheet or a piece of accounting software. Or even the back of an envelope. If your financial affairs are simple, don't over-complicate them.

A friend of mine who's just taken the *Leap!* proudly told me his accountant handles everything. That's fine if it's not costing him much (and it doesn't) but don't over-complicate it – you should be able to handle stuff like this yourself in its most simplistic terms. But however you do it, make sure it gets done. If you're not great with money and spreadsheets then do outsource to a relative, friend or accountant. As long as you have the information at your disposal, that is key. Because if you have messed up on a project and your costs have exceeded your earnings, you have a big problem, and the sooner you know about it, the better. If you know about it quick, you can fix it. If not, things are going to get messy.

Always look out for good deals and shop around for suppliers, get value for money and value-added service. Remember, *this is your money*; prudence and being resourceful need to be your mantra across all your life now.

21

On the cheap

So when it's your money it's different.

Why take a cab when a tube ride will save you money?

Why stay at that expensive conference hotel when you've found a cheaper one around the corner?

Sometimes it's difficult doing things on the cheap. International travel and conventions can get expensive so you need to be resourceful. A colleague and I decided that an invitation to a party in Cannes was not to be missed, but the town – especially during the Film Festival – is one of the most expensive cities on the planet. We shopped around, got a great deal train ticket to France and found a decent hotel where we shared a room in a cheaper alternative to the normal way of doing Cannes. We got there on the cheap, which matters when you're paying the expenses rather than putting in a claim to the accounts department.

The year earlier I'd taken a similar approach on a visit to that same town when I was co-managing a rock band. Midem is *the* event for networking new music and building relationships so we knew we had to be there. But we also knew we had to pay the convention fees and hotel and travel out of our own pockets. The first time I'd visited Cannes I'd been on client expenses and stayed at the Martinez; this time it was a basic apartment off Le Croisette – a sofa bed for me and a bedroom for my business partner. With drinks in hotel bars at 15 euros each, we couldn't do everything on the cheap, but we were a tiny business and we had no choice other than to be resourceful. We eschewed posh lunches at places to be seen for a quick lunch at McDonald's, saving our credit cards for a must-have dinner or that extortionate round of drinks.

So when you know that this is *the* opportunity to network your product, *the* place to be seen, you know you have to be there but you can also take that Cannes-do approach!

22

Different kinds of profit

Profit in business isn't *always* strictly financial – it's about a benefit. But whatever the benefit, make sure you profit from everything you do.

In my current portfolio I am working on a project on a pro-bono basis, which is a neat euphemism for doing something for nothing. It's a community project; hopefully I will enjoy the work and it's a nice bunch of people on the project team. So that's how I will profit.

And if it takes my career in a new direction or introduces me to some financially lucrative business, then it could become more profitable.

So when you are working for yourself, don't be too short-termist when it comes to evaluating work opportunities. It isn't always about short-term earnings.

You'll have to take 'the long view' on quite a few client relationships. Investing some time in a relationship with a new prospect, helping them out to tease them with something for free can be a successful tactic to getting them on board as a client so long as they don't take advantage of the situation. Those last seven words are the most important bit of that sentence. I always respect people and companies that have helped me out, especially where they have provided ideas or services for free, and I always remember them and repay their generosity where I can. Of course not everyone will take the same view, but it's a good starting point.

It's better to have a live and valuable contact with a business – even where they aren't a client yet – than not at all. You just have to work hard to turn that contact into a client. And some of that is about playing the waiting game.

I pitched for an assignment up against another guy. The other guy got it. The client asked me if I would mind spending an hour with the guy that got it, giving him – and them – the benefit of my ideas. A bit cheeky? But the client said they would appreciate any help I could give and they would then consider me for the next phase of the assignment. It's a risk but a risk I took. Did it pay off?

Well they've kept in touch and have asked me to pitch on another project …

23

What is 'core business' anyway?

This can be a tricky one; in order to be successful you need to be focused about what your offering is.

But in order to be successful you need to be open-minded about what you take on and enterprising in all you do. Diversification and generating multiple revenue streams is a good strategy because it's less risky than putting all your eggs in one basket. So long as you can juggle an eclectic portfolio without any part of it suffering.

The liberation of working for yourself is having no restrictions on your business style, portfolio or activities. As long as you can reconcile that liberation with focus, being more enterprising = greater success.

When I headed up a division within a larger company, I was in trouble if I strayed too far from 'core business'. When I reported at one board meeting that our biggest project had been producing some video content for a global brand, eyebrows were raised since producing video was not what we did. But I outsourced the video production; I personally looked after client relations and we employed all our in-house project management abilities to make sure it ran smoothly. In my books a successful project is a successful project. It uses the same disciplines and skills, whether you are producing a new product or producing a bunch of videos. That was my rationale for going off-piste, I'm not sure the board 'got it'. Until, that is, they saw the management accounts for that month and the healthy profit margin.

Then they got it.

24

Get a reward

Hopefully most clients will pay you fees to obtain services. Others may offer you equity stakes or profit share as part of a package. Some start-ups, since they are not cash rich, may offer you equity *in place of* fees.

I've had discussions with ventures where the founders have tempted me with percentage stakes. Percentage stakes are all well and good but 20% of nothing is still nothing, so be realistic about how – or actually *if* – you can turn the stake into cash.

It can be worth taking a risk if you get the right mix of equity and cash. When I was younger I was offered a job in a start-up as MD: a basic salary lower than my existing package plus a stake in the company. But back then salary was what turned me on; I didn't 'get' equity, I was hung up on negotiating a higher basic salary. Looking back, this venture could have been a great success and I could have benefited accordingly.

But that's quite a big 'could have', and you are always going to have to weigh up the risks. However attractive the opportunity – unless it's a not-for-profit client where I choose to work pro bono – I have a principle. There must be *some* fees as part of any project package. Business doesn't work on 'ifs' and 'coulds'.

25
Doing the sell

When you are job hunting you are told to have a CV. Most of them look the same with their similar formats and identical headings. Career histories mapped out, job titles and responsibilities spun to their potential, some candidates still including their education achievements as if that mattered. Fewer employers really care about what degree you got and they certainly aren't interested in whether you prefer scuba diving to skating. But they are interested in one thing: what it says about the candidate.

And when you start your own business, your credentials are your sales tools. So you need to create a professional summary:

! A sales document for your business.

! A punchy, brief biography.

! Or a document that sells YOU. Segment your career into project-based achievements, so it's the projects and clients that stand out rather than the roles you had.

! Or write your own career story, like a living obituary.

Don't pad it out. Keep it relevant. What you are, what you've done, for whom, what you offer, why you're different.

Whatever currency you choose, remember it's about *your story*, not a bunch of job titles. And people like to hear a good story.

When you think about ways of selling yourself, remember that you have to compete on factors other than price. Like ideas and experience. Because there are so many other companies out there that you are up against. The new economy has created a fragmented market full of small businesses offering seemingly similar services. Clients may assume that the quality of your work, service or product is good enough. So you'll have to compete on something else to make you stand out from the competition.

Clients will hire you because they like the experience of working with you; and they'll hire you because you have loads of good ideas that will benefit their brand or business.

So you need to be nice guys to deal with, and you have to have loads of good ideas.

And those are probably more important factors to focus on and to get right if you are going to be a success.

26

Keep in touch

Keeping in touch with clients and contacts is vital, reminding them you are there, keeping visible and staying on their radar so you are in the right place at the right time when an opportunity arises. It may be a cliché but 'right place, right time' continues to be a reason for winning business.

A timely 'keep in touch' email to a contact can result in some work: I fired off an email to an old colleague about some services my new business was providing and I got a call back later that day with a brief. I'd never have got the work if I hadn't been proactive in my communications.

Another time I sent a client a note of congratulations on winning an award and then suggested a communications initiative. They liked the idea and asked us to produce the initiative. Our enterprising and timely approach paid off. So keep abreast of news so you know what's going on in your contacts' business lives.

Others prefer to take a more laissez-faire attitude and wait for clients to contact them, but it's a competitive market out there and you risk losing out to someone more proactive than you. Being passive is not an option when it comes to business development.

There are some more formal ways you can keep in touch with contacts, prospects and clients: an email or hard copy newsletter, viral communication, letter or brochure. But some of those ad hoc less formal initiatives are often more effective: a congratulations card on a new business win, sending a cutting that may interest them or a feature about their sector you saw on the TV news. I've also sent cards to clients at the end of a big project, sent business books that have inspired me to clients at Christmas, even a book of *Frasier* scripts to an old client who loves the show. It keeps you memorable.

Just make sure the recipient doesn't misunderstand your motives. When I was a young executive, I was so inspired by Tom Peters' book *Liberation Management* (1992, Pan Books) that I gave a copy to my boss with some annotations of chapters he might find interesting. Despite my good intentions he must have thought I was trying to tell him something about his management skills; he never said anything about that book.

So keep in touch, but keep it relevant.

27

Quick and ready

In the *scrambled up world* you have to think quickly and be ready to react instantly. Many pieces of business are won just by being able to react fast enough.

I had just launched a marketing business and was meeting a contact. He asked if I could introduce him to a big advertising agency as he wanted to run a newspaper ad later that week. It was late Monday morning; he wanted the ad in that Thursday's newspaper. I phoned around my contacts. Both agencies I called said they'd love to meet my client the next week or the week after and 'sit down and plan a campaign'. No one could service my client's instant requirements to turn around an ad and get it booked in two working days. No one would do it; it wasn't in the rules – they just didn't work like that.

So I decided to do it myself. I called my designers and contacted a media buyer. I took a risk and paid for the ad space up front, and we delivered. The ad worked and 18 months later this was my biggest client, booking and producing four or five ads every month. Traditional business practice was not reactive enough, and my quick response had paid off.

Similarly, one summer, a client I had been courting for a long time got in touch. Did we want to pitch for a job? If so, we needed to be in town the next day for a meeting. We went in for a brief on the Friday and they wanted us to present back to them on the Thursday. That's three clear working days. Most other agencies would have said three days was not enough time to turn around ideas, especially in mid August when everyone's on holiday. But if you are going to be enterprising, there is no other option but to be quick and ready.

We won the pitch.

28

Brand power

Once you start a business, make sure you build a good brand. Branding is not about pretty logos, it's about your whole ethos and what your proposition means to the marketplace.

Simply, your brand is what makes your business different, special and compelling. So it's important to get it right.

Those tangible outlets of your brand are also important: your logo, your website, your communications. All those bits that 'touch' your audience. And the challenge is to ensure they reflect your business personality because this is what will influence clients to buy your services.

So ask yourself this: does my brand identity and website reflect what makes my business special? If not, it should do.

In the last three years my business has had four 'looks' and that's because the business has changed and so the brand needs to reflect that. Much of my recent business offering has seen us refreshing clients' business and marketing strategies so it's important to practise what you preach. It's a changing market and we need to change too. Even a world-famous brand like Virgin doesn't stand still. It may have the same *V* logo but straplines, ad campaigns and messages constantly change. The brand principles stay the same.

And once you have built a successful brand you can leverage that power to grow your business in other sectors, united by the same brand promises. A client of mine who built a progressive mortgage business is going to apply the same values about what makes his business different to other sectors.

Ultimately, brand success is about your shop window on the market. If you have an existing relationship with the marketplace selling one product or service then why not sell other products and services to the same people? If you can achieve that without diluting or jeopardizing your core activity, then it can be a good way of growing your business.

So many offerings are the same. So success is about differentiation. Make sure you are different by ensuring your offering, your marketing and your message all exude personality.

Ultimately success is about *sales*, so maximize the brand to generate multiple revenue streams and make those client relationships sweat.

29
Reinvent yourself

Your brand identity isn't the only thing that's going to change. You'll have to reinvent your business in other areas too to reflect a rapidly changing business climate. Often and quickly. Be prepared to rewrite the rules as you go.

It can be unsettling but you'll have to reinvent things like:

1 What you do.

2 How you describe it.

3 Your business model and how you make money.

4 Your client base.

5 How you stand out from the competition.

6 Your product range, creating new and improved offerings.

The ability to reinvent yourself is one of the key tools you need. Reinvention to stay ahead of the market with great ideas and products that the market wants. That's the trick. Clients have to reinvent and change themselves in order to survive and succeed so they will want to see evidence of this in their suppliers too.

There is no point operating under unwieldy or unworkable business models. If your business model is broken or unsustainable and you've given it a decent try, don't wait too long before changing it.

For those of us who have experienced a technological revolution in the workplace, we've had to embrace change, and quickly. Mobile phones, email, the Internet. Doing business quicker and in more demanding circumstances than our parents' generation. Using computers was not something I learnt as a kid or at school; it was something I had to learn in the workplace like many of my working generation. And, of course, there was no option but to embrace change and embrace technology. You have no choice; you cannot stand still. So you can't afford to say, I'm not going to change or learn something new.

Because every project, assignment and gig is like a movie. You have to play a different role, with different co-stars, for different pay.

Every time.

A different director (that's the client) and a whole set of different challenges; you hope it will be blockbuster but you never know until it's released.

And it can get tedious. The only thing that's constant is you.

So learn to embrace and enjoy change.

30
Living off your latest gig

When you work for an employer you live off your collective achievements; you're an ambassador not just for your own achievements but also you wave the corporate flag for the whole company. And clients may like you because they like the company rather than because they like you. On the plus side, you get the chance to bask in that collective corporate glory of feats that have nothing to do with you.

When you are on your own, it's just you. And you are only as good as your latest gig.

You can't dine out on what you did 12 or 18 months ago. Clients want to know what are you doing now; what did you last do? So you always need a current, relevant and signature project.

What is a signature project? The total expression of you professionally. Something you are proud of, something you can shout about. A project that is a good example of what you do, of how you do it, and the value it brings to your client.

Identify your current, relevant and signature projects and shout about them.

31
Picking your team

When you work for yourself you may not walk into a big office every morning but the chances are you still have co-workers and you may need to build a team of freelancers and suppliers to deliver a project.

These team members may not work for you in the traditional sense but you still need to pick them carefully – because they are effectively an extension of you and your business, which means you all need to share some values to make sure the project has your stamp on it from end to end. And the challenge is to keep them under control.

Since they're not on your payroll, your team's loyalty will inevitably be measured by what you pay them or what they perceive the earning potential to be from their relationship with you. Unless they just really like you (which is a possibility).

And how much you pay your team may be your only leverage in the relationship to encourage them to act and work as you would like. And if that's all it is, that you are paying their invoice, that is not a bad motivation for all of you.

If possible pick team members not just on ability and price but also on attitude and working practices. Will they turn projects around quickly? Will they respond to communications promptly? How will they act in a client meeting? An IT systems expert may be good at his job but how good is he going to be at client-facing? If you are unsure, leave that side of the project with you.

If in doubt, instinct is your best tool. Because often you have to make quick decisions in business. And that means being able to make a judgement without knowing too much about someone. Never underestimate an hour with a potential team member over a beer or a glass of wine. It's like a first date; you can learn a lot about someone in that first meeting and decide whether you want a relationship or whether you don't fancy them at all …

32
Get some personalities

When you're picking the team, it's also important to know they are going to have the right mix, not only in hard graft, but also in personality. One of my mentors said he utilized the 'dinner party test' when hiring people; would the candidate be some-one he'd be happy having dinner with? Did he warm to their personality?

I am not sure how realistic that criterion is – I have hired some people who were really good at their jobs, but I would not have liked the idea of dinner with all of them. But they do need to have the right kind of outlook.

I worked at a company that had an innovative spirit; its team was young, progressive and shared a sense of personality. That was what gave it an edge. Most of us liked a few drinks so we socialized together on a Friday night, sharing a few bottles of wine in the boardroom. Those kinds of get-togethers were great fun but more importantly it was what helped define the company spirit, that shared experience. When the company grew and more executives started hiring – rather than the founders – that personality criteria diluted and managers hired people who were just good at their jobs, not people who would also fit in. And this was a mistake. Diversity in a team is good but you need to retain that common spirit and that means hiring people with Personality.

And your team has to have personality if your business is going to stand out.

33
Going naked

People in business get nervous about stripping away the corporate layers that support and protect them in their jobs: suits, offices, assistants. Take the layers away and you have raw materials, raw talent and self-sufficient enterprise. And when you

Leap! you have to strip yourself back to those bare essentials, to try to act self-sufficiently even if you don't need to. It'll make you more enterprising.

But going 'naked' is for many a frightening experience. I know a small business that doesn't make money. I can see – in a *flash* – what they are doing wrong. The company has a headcount of eight but not the revenues to match. That says one thing to me.

GO LEAN!

NOW!

Not in three months. Not in six months. Not after the third year of the owner's five-year plan. But now. This week. Today.

But the owner's background is in big business and she has built herself a micro-empire, taking comfort from people, juniors around her. Deferring and delegating to others. Strip it down and she'll worry what signal that sends to the marketplace. If it downsizes, clients may think it's failed. But the fact is that it's not making money anyway and to survive it'll need some radical re-engineering. And that means you have to be brave enough to strip the layers away to examine what's right, what's wrong and what needs changing.

It's like a musician. You've got to be able to play acoustic, without all that amplification and band behind you.

You've got to be able to cut it solo.

Part Three
SUCCESS

If enterprise is about getting there, success is about staying there.

There's no definitive 'How To Be Successful' guide once your business is up and running.

But there are some really important considerations in terms of how you stand out in the marketplace and how you maximize opportunities. When you're working for yourself it's a competitive world out there and you need to stay ahead of the game in every way you can: providing added value to clients and staying fresh and in demand.

You also need to stay focused, not just when starting out but also when delivering your ideas, your plan, your business. Because without delivery of ideas, you can't have success.

1

Starting up and finishing up

To be successful you have to be a completer, i.e. a starter *and* a finisher.

If you're someone who has buckets of great ideas, great – but do you have the ability and the philosophy to complete them? If not, you might need a partner. And that's why partnerships are so effective – one person is the creative one, the other the businesswoman; one the product developer, the other the sales expert. So you need to be honest about your own limitations.

Coming up with genius ideas is critical but being able to deliver is just as essential. Take a look at your current bunch of ideas and projects – can you complete them all, take them to fruition?

If not, how not, where not? Can you identify a business partner or resource to fill that vacuum? A top salesperson, a numbers guy or an outsourced solution? You may need to outsource a whole range of disciplines from finance to design, IT to marketing.

Outsourcing is a great option for the small entrepreneur but you can never outsource responsibility or accountability. You and only you take the responsibility for implementation; it's your business and you need to have the overview. And *you* need the systems and structures to make sure everything is done, that the job is executed on time, that the invoice is sent, suppliers are paid and that the marketing has been done.

Remember that the notion of a great idea is just not enough to pay the bills. Delivery of projects and ideas is where it's at, in the details, in the execution, in making a difference to client cultures and businesses.

Ideas may have wowed the client in the presentation but it's the effectiveness of those ideas on the shop floor, in the market-place that will measure the success of that idea.

So it doesn't matter if you came up with a genius concept for that product launch. Instead, it's a question of: did it do the job? How many new sales did it deliver? That's what counts.

2

Do you have what it takes?

Do you have **IT**?

Successful business leaders will often talk about the *entre-preneurial spirit* that made them what they are. Business commentators and politicians also talk about the importance of that ingredient for a vibrant economy.

But what is 'entrepreneurial spirit'? And do you have what it takes to make you a success? That is the inevitable $60,000 question.

'Entrepreneurial spirit' is what *Leap!* is all about; it's the confidence, ambition and ability to deliver successful projects, to create a profitable activity from scratch. To take an idea and turn that into something tangible that pays the bills. And that's quite a powerful package; that brainpower focused on success.

But you don't need to be head of a global business to be blessed with entrepreneurial spirit. Many of us have it. The single mother who holds down a part-time job to earn enough for her kids; the schoolgirl who has a paper round and sells her handmade jewellery in the playground; the trainee sales guy who's pulling out the stops to prove himself. They are all driven by the desire to better themselves, by the desire to succeed.

It's not a magic potion; you can't buy it online. You might not have it from day one, but it's the fuel to keep your business going; to have the ability to see ideas through and to persevere despite knock-backs and obstacles.

It's instinctive, and you'll need it to succeed.

3
You don't need big tools

When you start a new small business it's easy to assume you need infrastructure: people/hardware/desks/offices. The conventional tools of running a business.

But all you actually need is a laptop, a phone, a bunch of ideas and a decent business card. That's all the dot.com entrepreneurs ever had in Silicon Valley, sitting at their laptops in coffee shops. The founders of Google didn't have an office when they started out, just a garage.

It's not about being risk averse, it's about being flexible. Without the burden of staff on the payroll and bricks and mortar premises, it's easier to change, easier to adapt quickly to changing circumstances, whether losing a client or starting a new project. You don't have to staff up or down in the traditional sense with all the baggage that brings. Virtual working can be more effective and more efficient for a rapidly changing world. Sometimes clients may expect you to have 'proper offices' but increasingly they may respect your offering if you don't – for a start, you'll be more cost effective than those competitors who have to carry bigger overheads.

So keep it simple and save on those overheads.

And build a business on great ideas, not bricks and mortar.

4

Business doesn't come in a flat pack

There's no such thing as an 'everything you need' guide to business. A start-up business does not come in a flat-pack with a set of instructions.

For a start, there are no instructions.

Sure, there are books and resources that can help inspire and steer your ideas. You can learn accounting and you can try to learn sales but there's no quick fix for learning business success. Last year I went to an exhibition for start-ups. In the foyer a woman was handing out carrier bags full of promotional literature and telling passers by, 'Inside is everything you need to start a business.'

Well, whatever you do need to have success in business, it certainly doesn't come in a carrier bag.

With so much advice and information out there on business and enterprise it can be hard to know what to follow and what to ignore.

There's so much crap out there, you just have to trust your intuition. I was leafing through a business magazine the other day and it had a piece on how to dress for business. It said, always wear sensible shoes and men should wear dark-coloured socks.

??!!

What bo*****s. This is 2008, not 1988. No one's going to judge you on that. A business book (billed as 'an international bestseller') I browsed said a business dress code should be 'no jeans, no trainers'. But like nightclub rules that allow the yob wearing the suit in whilst the well-behaved guy in his designer jeans stays out, it's hopelessly flawed.

Too many people starting out focus on the wrong details: an over-elaborate brochure, a complicated PowerPoint presentation and, yes, sensible shoes and dark socks.

You have to keep it simple: do you have a viable business proposition? Do you have good ideas? How are you going to sell it? Where are your customers?

And wear whatever colour socks you feel like.

5

The six-point business plan

Friends and associates who work for big corporations are forever working on three- or five-year business plans, projecting the future of their business units or divisions. In this new world of work, even a 12-month plan can be a challenge; if your business is constantly evolving, it's tough to forecast. Similarly, if your business is influenced by technological development, you'll struggle to predict how technology itself will change in 12 months.

All you can do is throw a bunch of figures into a spreadsheet and find a way – some way – of meeting them.

For the scrambled up entrepreneur, whilst banks and investors may need five-year business plans, it's far more likely you can't project beyond six months, let alone 12.

So don't waste time on a five-year plan; you'll only change it in six months anyway.

And that's one of the perks of life once you've taken the *Leap!*. You don't need to get bogged down with forecasts and projections. Just have a gut-based plan and go for it.

Planning your business should be instinctive. And that means you don't need an accountancy qualification to succeed.

So the best game plan is probably not to have one; flexibility is the key in a constantly changing marketplace.

Try a bullet-point business plan – six bullet points (no more, no less) of your business objectives for the next six months:

1   What one thing makes your business different, makes it stand out?

2   How are you going to sell your product or service to clients? Who are your target clients?

3 How are you going to keep your costs down?

4 How are you going to maximize revenues?

5 How are you going to deal with competition?

6 How can you grow the business? What will you need to deliver that growth?

This isn't a business plan of financial projections. It's not for your bank manager or accountant. But it can be the *basis* of your business strategy.

6

It's who you know (of course)

Getting a job or getting new business has *always* been about who you know. All my business interests have been founded on who I know. Indeed, I cannot think of a single piece of business in the last year or so that has not been connected by a direct contact of mine:

1   one client was my wife's ex-boss;

2   one client was my friend's boss;

3   one client was my friend's former colleague;

4   one client was my former employer;

5   a number of clients are my friends.

Just as the lines between work and leisure have crumbled, so too have the distinctions between personal and professional relationships. Friends have become clients and business associates. Business associates and clients have become friends. It's never been a done deal where I got business via friends; in every case where I have worked with a friend, I was appointed on merit, sometimes in a competitive pitch. It's just that the friendship got me the initial introduction.

Once you have made the *Leap!* you need to be confident and prepared to do 'The Sell' to all your contacts, including friends and family. Because you are always going to get better results from warm contacts than cold ones. Spending all day targeting people you don't know will always be very tough; targeting people you do know will be more fruitful. Because even if they do not want to buy, they may have friends or colleagues who do.

If you are struggling to drum up business, write down a list of your contacts who can help you win business. Think which ones can be clients, which can introduce business to you, and which can help spread the word.

Then consider the currency of communication for each, how you can approach them with your business sell.

Remember that you *are* your 'black book' (or whatever colour book it is). You become defined by your contacts, by who you know.

Never underestimate the value of your contacts. There was a time when I made the mistake of doing just this. An associate of mine suggested we exchange our contacts so we could target each other's for new business. A case of 'you show me yours, I'll show you mine'. I showed her mine; she didn't 'get round' to showing me hers.

7

Getting connected

Graduates have career plans. HR directors and line managers fill out appraisal forms and map out 12-month objectives and milestones. But for most of us, our career path is much more scrambled up.

My career history runs something like this:

1   First job – working Saturdays for uncle's friend who ran a gift shop and record label.

2 Next a part-time job working at local radio station. Experience in job No. 1 helped me get job No. 2.

3 Job No. 2 helped me get on a college media course. Did a college attachment to a TV production company. TV company hired me when I left university – job No. 3.

4 Met bloke at job No. 3 who hired me to work at an events and music company – job No. 4.

5 The husband of the office manager at job No. 3 was a director of a radio company. He hired me – job No. 5.

6 Seven years later I went independent and my first clients were the radio company (job No. 5) and one of its shareholders. Another client was a contact from job No. 4.

7 Etc.

I once doodled a chart of my network of contacts and it was completely interlinked; my career history is built on the people I know and there were surprising interrelationships between contacts who I knew through multiple points of contact. Forget six degrees of separation; my professional network is more closely connected.

Think why social and professional networking websites are so valuable: everyone likes to work with someone who is connected.

Plot your own network of contacts and you may spot opportunities that you hadn't noticed before.

8

Get yourself a mentor

It will be lonely if you are a one-person business. You might spend hours – days even – on a decision, struggling to find a solution to a problem, to work out the answer. Or trying to perfect a document, report, proposal or product.

So you need a sounding board, or even a few sounding boards. Someone else to give you that fresh perspective, to stop you getting stale and also to help with those details like spotting that typo in your presentation. Your flatmate, your partner, an old colleague, someone you can call or email.

I have a few. My wife to give me a second opinion; a copywriter mate to look over those proposals and documents; an old mate of mine to give me an honest view on a problem or decision; a former client and now friend to advise on those difficult financial decisions; and an old mate to bully me to make sure I am writing this book (thanks, David).

If you have a partner in your life they will help you take the *Leap!* providing the moral and financial support. The moral support to say 'yes, you *can* do it' and the financial support to say 'yes, we *can* pay the rent this month'.

Financial support will be invaluable because when you take the *Leap!* any safety net is welcome, so if you can lean on another revenue stream – great. If your husband/boyfriend/wife/girlfriend will happily underwrite you, you can take a risk with your new business idea. Moral support is just as important – from someone to have a moan to, to being a surrogate co-worker, it helps.

You'll find it valuable assembling an informal 'advisory team' of clients, friends and suppliers that know you and know your business. Just make sure there is something in it for them, like you return the favour. There has to be a lot of reciprocity – you don't want to be a drain on a friendship or relationship.

However impressive a one-person business unit can be in generating ideas and bringing in business, you're going to need help. And when you're struggling with something, two heads are better than one.

Listen to others and recognize that you need others to mentor, guide and help out. So if you're taking the *Leap!* remember you may be self-sufficient but you can't do all of it on your own.

9

Polymaths have all the fun

In business there are specialists and there are generalists. Those that are expert in one discipline and do that all their lives; and those that have more transferable skills and can be successful in a number of disciplines and industries.

Society and business tend to favour specialists. People are writers, recruitment consultants, bankers, lawyers, estate agents, brand managers, whatever. If we want advice we talk to a specialist.

But we don't always know how to deal with professionals who have experience in a variety of disciplines and sectors. At worst, we see it as a weakness or a sign of lack of focus. In fact it makes for more interesting dynamics if people mix up different disciplines.

For many people who have taken the *Leap!* they find they do a variety of 'stuff' to earn a living. I have always thrived on a multi-discipline portfolio – I'd be bored of a single-track career and that's in contrast to convention.

But dump convention. In this New Economy it's a meritocracy – you really can do whatever you want, and if you want to change tack from being an accountant to launching an online clothing company, you can. There's no such thing as a formal career path any more.

You can either do the same thing your whole career or you can be promiscuous, take some risks and live the polymath life.

Remember that specialists are perceived as more hireable than generalists. Whilst being a generalist should make you a more saleable commodity because you have extra disciplines, skills and experience at your disposal, that's a concept clients and employers struggle with. I have solid experience in seven or eight sectors and disciplines. It's this broad portfolio that has given me the stimulation and tools to be enterprising and earn a living. But it is a more complex sell and that means clients don't always 'get it'.

Everyone likes a focused professional; some struggle with the notion that this guy might be very good at seven or eight things rather than exceptional at one. It's not easy being a polymath.

But then, no one ever said that working this way was going to be easy.

10

What do you do again?

Like it or not, we are defined by what we do, by what our job is.

'What do you **do**?' goes the dinner party question. 'What does your new girlfriend **do**?' ask your friends. 'And what do you **do**?' asks the radio phone-in host. I have never liked the question, mainly because I don't have an easy answer: I do – and have always done – a mixture of 'stuff'. My wife hates being asked what her husband does for the same reason, because it's complex. If only I had a conventional single-discipline job it would be easier. I'm a lawyer! I'm a vet!

But as we've seen, increasingly we get more complex answers:

> 'I am an account manager and also a photographer. But as I work at home I also help out with childcare for my daughter. And I am running a small Internet business with my wife.'

And:

> 'I do loads of stuff. I run a mortgage company; I also have a property development business and I own a stake in a travel agency.'

Others want to know what job you do because it defines you, but of course without knowing the full story, they still don't know the person. Knowing Sarah's a lawyer and that Alan's a dentist tells us nothing about their story or personality. I think other interests could so much better define people. 'I love vodka, watching Japanese films and I'd love to be a gardener if only I could quit my boring job' says so much more.

But for the moment social convention remains, 'What do you do?'

And my answer is: 'I live in the very *scrambled up world of work*.'

11

Lucky breaks

Whatever people say about why they have been successful, remember that apart from hard graft one of the biggest contributors to success is LUCK.

! Luck in meeting the right person.

! Luck in knowing the right person.

! Luck in spotting the opportunity.

! Luck of being in the right place at the right time.

Often, winning business is not the result of a finely tuned direct marketing campaign or a well-planned strategy. You are more likely to get a lead from a bloke you'd nearly forgotten who you once worked with ten years ago. Charlie was one of those. He was finance director of a client I'd worked with way back but he tracked me down and asked if I wanted to be considered for an opportunity. In my book that's lucky.

I was early for a train and happened to browse a magazine at a news stand I wouldn't have normally seen and I spotted an article about a development that was of great value to my client. That was lucky.

You can't create luck; there's no business formula for it. You just have to hope you get lucky.

12
Facing up

You can do so much business without seeing anyone. Once a business relationship starts you will have meetings with a client but, beyond that, so much is done virtually, on email and by telephone that you could go weeks or months without seeing a client. You routinely provide a service to them, and send an invoice month in, month out. You have some new creative treatments to show them but you're both busy so you just email them a PDF. It's so easy not to meet, you just have to make the effort and take the initiative to ensure you do, to sit down face to face.

Put regular meetings in with a client to review projects or business. I had a big client and I scheduled regular meetings every couple of weeks. Sometimes it was just 15 minutes, others were a couple of hours, but whatever the duration it was worth doing. Having a catch up, sometimes taking a brief in the boardroom, other times a coffee in a café. Keeping in touch, staying visible. Since so much of business success is about right time, right place it's worth being across the table with a client whenever you can, so you can say, 'I can help you with that project' or 'I might have an idea to grow your business.' Also, it makes you more memorable and less disposable.

The same applies to project teams. With a virtual team of members working all over the place from their respective workplaces, it can seem a hassle to get together but it does make such a difference to results and productivity. In a room, in a coffee shop, in a bar, the team dynamic will be real and they'll be an energy you can't achieve on email or by phone. The kind of energy that's essential for any project to succeed.

13
Don't waste time

Inevitably when you first take the *Leap!* or start a business you will spend a lot of time on things that don't instantly yield a return. And that is fine – that's business; you can't spend *every* waking hour directly making money. You'll try – but you can't. But similarly, time is precious and you have to make sure you don't waste it.

Don't waste time on projects that are going nowhere. Don't waste time on relationships that will go nowhere.

How do you know if they are a waste of time?

With time, experience and instinct. But when you're busy it's easy to get swept along with the momentum of a new relationship or prospect. You have to stand back and ask yourself:

At some stage, whenever that may be, is this activity going to result in me sending an invoice to someone?

Ask that all the time; get it tattooed on your arm.

So time management is important, you have to put in the hours and optimize that time to invest in your business. The key is in your approach. I have spent a whole day focused on some task or some challenge, sitting at my desk and getting nowhere. Then I have gone to a coffee shop for one hour, just 60 minutes, and achieved so very much. It's amazing what you can achieve in a smaller space of time. It's all about a focused attitude and a pragmatic approach.

Whatever you do, don't waste time. Ask yourself, do I really need to be looking at Facebook and YouTube right now?

So find a currency or a coffee shop that works for you. If you are worried about making the most of a blank day, then segment it as you would if you had a bunch of meetings. Earmark different time slots for different tasks to ensure you optimize your time.

Use your thinking time effectively and successfully. As you go through the week, ask yourself, what have I achieved or done this morning?

And if you don't have an answer, if you can't be accountable for your time, then you have something else. And that's called a problem.

14

Ideas, ideas, ideas

When you are managing your own time you need to have space for ideas generation. If you are really busy it may not seem like a priority but having good ideas is at the heart of any successful business. And you're unlikely to have the big idea if you don't give yourself some space.

You can't always manufacture the right criteria for coming up with great ideas. But some things will help:

! A different environment away from your desk.

! Your mind temporarily cleared of your to-do list.

! Away from distractions of phone and email.

! A blank sheet of paper and a list of objectives.

If you are struggling with the process, focus on producing a tangible outcome: a plan, proposal, a strategy. Or just a list. The notion of ideas generation is so very abstract it will help to put your thoughts down on paper.

Seek inspiration in whatever way works for you. And then ideas will come.

I often sit in a coffee shop and give myself a couple of ideas to develop or challenges to consider in that session. I never cease to be impressed by what that format can fuel. My notes become the foundation for what I will do back at my desk. Many of these very chapters started as theme or subject headings scribbled on paper with some notes alongside each of them. A lot of that was done during coffee-shop thinking time. Back at my desk I did the writing bit. And by having a framework like that I ensured that I optimized my time because there was a focus and accountability to each day.

Sometimes a focused session will yield success; other times you'll have those eureka moments in the middle of the night, on holiday, cleaning your teeth. So you might be better off going on holiday to clean your teeth in the middle of the night and wait for all those ideas to flow!

Either way, success is going to depend on how good you are at ideas. Thinking of new ways of doing stuff, an initiative to wow a client, or a new way of earning money.

So make time for them.

15

The importance of scribbles on little scraps of paper

When you're taking the *Leap!* you'll find your brain is working overtime with ideas and thoughts. And if it's not, it bloody well should be.

Email, laptops, BlackBerries, PDAs are all very well for capturing and documenting ideas. But don't underestimate the importance of everyday scribbles in journals, notebooks, on scraps of paper, edges of newspapers and even beer mats.*

It's in these kind of places I have documented some of my best ideas. I'm forever downloading my thoughts, ideas and actions on to scraps of paper and there's something attractive about the simplicity of the medium that can be the catalyst for great ideas. It's also something that can lay unobtrusively by the side of the bed to note down those midnight eureka moments.

---

* Once I prepared for a meeting on a beer mat and took it into my meeting with the boss. He looked at me strangely and said, 'You can use a notebook, you know.' But the beer mat captured everything it needed to: a couple of bullet points of a great idea. It would have lost its simplicity on a notepad.

A scribble on paper is a great ideas generator; indeed, they are all the raw materials I need. I am at my happiest with:

! A pen.

! A blank piece of paper.

! Clarity and some damn great ideas.

And as a result I never have that moment where I go, 'What *was* that great idea I had?' because it's down on paper somehow, somewhere. Because if successful business is about having great ideas you need to make sure you capture those ideas. And whatever the merits of digital storage, you can't beat a scribble on a scrap of paper.

After all, this is where this chapter started.

16
Learn to say 'no'

Often it's hard to say no.

No one likes letting someone down but in business it's important to be honest and direct. Whether you need to terminate a supplier arrangement, change a team member or review a new venture, you need to have the courage to flag up concerns or questions.

I was working with a new contact on a start-up idea. I wouldn't be hands-on but would be a co-director, put time and a small amount of money in and take a profit share. It seemed a no-brainer and a viable business.

But I was worried about time, about spreading myself too thin, about diluting my focus in my core business by my involvement in another venture.

We'd been talking and planning the business for a couple of months and then we were both really busy and had a hiatus. And that hiatus gave me the space to have a think about the venture and it was then I had concerns. We had come a long way and I hated to change my mind but I didn't feel committed to a proper partnership with all the passion and responsibility it requires.

She's a really nice woman but I had to disappoint her and pull out.

But it's better to be honest and disappoint now then wait until you have done loads of work and then it's too late or too damaging to pull out.

17

Know when to shut up!

When it comes to business communications, keep it short, keep it simple and keep it to the point.

When I write proposals to clients I always try to keep it to one page. No reams of stuff they don't need to know. Just the essentials. The same with presentations; don't waste time telling the client what they already know. I could have used 80,000 words to communicate the message of this book but I figured I might do it more effectively with just 40,367.

Keep every part of your business communications brief, punchy and relevant.

The same applies to pitches and meetings. Winning business is about demonstrating to the client your understanding of their business and their product. There's a fine line between empathy and sycophancy:

! Don't waste time telling them what they already know.

! Don't witter on about some self-indulgent anecdote that you think is relevant and funny. Because it probably isn't relevant and they definitely won't find it funny.

! Just communicate some damn good ideas.

Effective presentations are not about how well you perform. They are not about flash PowerPoint presentations or slides projected on a big screen; they are just about communication. My best currency is to sit down around a table and present a bunch of ideas in collaboration with the client. By all means demonstrate you have done your homework but show them some respect. They are inevitably time-poor. They have sat through loads of other – similar – presentations. So strip yours down to the basics, be different, be concise and don't talk *at* them. It's just as important to *listen* to them as it is to *talk*.

If you're getting negative signals or body language cut it short and seek feedback. Pitches have been lost by not being to the point. So don't bore the pants off your audience, excite them.

And remember, you've got to know when to shut up!

18

Value + value

What's all this talk of 'added value'?

It's a competitive world out there and you have to stand out, be different from the rest, so your proposition to a client needs to be 'value-added'. And you have to stay value-added to retain clients rather than lose them.

What value can you offer? All the obvious stuff like:

1   Great service.

2   At a good price.

3   A nice way of doing business.

But to be value-added you need to offer some of the non-obvious stuff:

1   Live and breathe your client's culture, make suggestions and be prepared to make contributions to them about their business, sometimes free of charge.

2   Build great relationships with them, connecting with people at all levels, not just with the woman that signs the cheques but also the guys on reception.

3   Make doing business together really easy; think of ways where the whole process can be made easier for them. Then it'll be easier for you too.

4   Respond to the non-obvious requests from clients about what they like and why they like working with you.*

---

* One new client asked me if I could change the size of my font on my emails. An odd response. But I did it – whatever turns your client on …

Remember never to stay still but keep moving, one step ahead of the client. Second guess how market changes will affect their business and make suggestions or formulate ideas to help them grow.

It's easy to get complacent with client relations, especially when you've worked together for a long time. Even if it's a project that seemingly 'looks after itself' make sure you pick up the phone. Keep in touch, staying active and interested in both the client and the project. Because there's no such thing as a project that looks after itself.

And if you don't strive to add value, you can bet your competitor will. And that could lose you the business.

19
Don't do mediocrity

Make sure you always over-deliver in your service and approach to clients and targets.

A mission to 'under-promise and over-deliver' is worth following. Tell the client you will get them that proposal by Friday and send it Wednesday. Throw in some extra deliverables that they weren't expecting when you deliver the project – give them more than they are paying for. It's sometimes easy to impress, to surprise.

Four weeks ago I asked a client of mine for some information about the configuration of their website. My client fired off an email to the web company posing the question. Four weeks later we don't have an answer. It was a simple question. The web company says they have passed the enquiry to their sales department. No response.

That's a bad sign for business. I would have fired them.

I was in the reception of a potential supplier the other day and overhead a conversation when a customer arrived to collect an order. It wasn't ready. But the client needed it for a store opening today; he had booked the photographer, everything was lined up. The supplier shrugged his shoulders: 'Well, these things happen,' he said, 'its sod's law'. There was no apology, no sharp intake of breath, no understanding of what it meant for the client. The supplier didn't even shift in his seat; he just didn't get it. Their poor attitude surprised me, but what surprised me more was that they seemingly run a successful business. But I won't work with them now.

It's a competitive market out there – clients don't need to tolerate mediocrity; they can move on to a new supplier, so make sure you don't do mediocrity. Ever.

20

Consume the world of your client

In super-serving your client, live and breathe their world.

Visit and inhabit their environments. Act like their customers do, read their advertisements, look through their trade press, critique their stores, interact with their staff, visit their websites, evaluate their branding, telephone their call centre and experience their customer service. Tell them what's good and what's bad. Without being asked.

Know what the client's doing or done. Prepare and research like mad. On their website and annual report. Google them, check out the relevant trade press, interviews. Who are their competitors, what do you perceive to be the challenges? If they have shares, buy a couple of shares in them, show you care!

It will give you an edge.

It's so obvious that people forget to do it.

I had a client in retail so I used to look at *Retail Week* magazine. Whilst I didn't read it cover to cover I did get a sense of the issues in the marketplace that were relevant to my client.

Recently I had a meeting with a supplier who's been providing some services to one of my clients for a couple of years. We were talking about my client. 'Have you been in one of their stores?' I asked. 'No,' the supplier replied. OK, they were my direct client, not his, but he was ten minutes from their store; it would have been so easy for him to make a visit but he'd never thought of it. That didn't impress.

Once I had a chain of bingo clubs as a client and after I'd been to head office for a meeting, a colleague and I would go to the local bingo club and play a game, soak up the atmosphere, live and breathe that brand. It always surprised the staff – two guys in suits turning up to play bingo in the middle of the afternoon may have looked an odd sight.

But how could we have done our jobs if we didn't consume our client's product? I would never work with a supplier or agency that hadn't bothered to consume my offering. The market is just too competitive; you have to show your passion and your willingness to consume their world.

21

Here's to a damn good lunch!

Lunch can be such a valuable currency in business development and networking: a format to do a lot of different things:

! Catching up with an old colleague.

! Keeping in touch with a client.

! Courting a target.

! Picking someone's brain.

! Maintaining a contact with someone you met at a conference.

It's neutral territory, it's less formal, it's out of the office and it can be more focused, so it's a great format for communication.

Lunch might be good for a lot of things but it's not good for taking a detailed brief or making a presentation. Do that bit first and then have lunch. A colleague and I once took a client out for dinner and gave him the presentation at the table. A bad move. Much better to give him the presentation first and then talk the details through over dinner. Similarly, trying to write too many notes over a lunch is not a good idea – stay focused on your guest and make your notes in the cab/on the tube afterwards. Because like any good business meeting a lunch is about communication. It can still be a really valuable forum for striking a deal, finding out some useful information or winning a piece of business but try to leave the paperwork under the table.

Meeting a client or contact for a glass of wine can be so valuable; some quality time at the end of the working day. When they are in a relaxed environment with a glass of something they are likely to be less guarded and more open about their views, their needs. As participants relax, you will see a different side of them and the creative juices will start flowing. At bars and tables this is where the really serious bits of business can happen.

Many of the best deals, plans hatched and ideas formulated were over a pint in a pub or a meal in a restaurant. So make sure you have an entertainment budget. It's more important than your paperclip budget.

22

Think ahead

The closest thing I have to a rule is that I prepare for every meeting by thinking ahead. I know it may sound obvious but in a busy workload it can easily get overlooked. For each meeting I ensure I have thought about what I need to contribute, discuss or find out. This may be in a typed-up one-pager or a scribble of some bullet points in a notepad. The prep may take me two days, two hours or two minutes.

But it is good practice. If you want to make sure you come across well in a meeting – prepare. A busy client or colleague who has not had time to think about the meeting in advance may flounder as you confidently go through what needs to be discussed and take the upper hand. Whichever party holds the agenda holds the power for the duration of that meeting.

It's so simple but so many people lose focus. They get busy or distracted. They don't think ahead. They have a meeting in their diary and turn up with no prior thoughts. But in this world there is no room for any passengers, and there's no space for sitting back. I can think of tens of meetings I've been to where participants don't actually participate. And worse, you ask them what their view is and they don't have anything to say because they haven't thought about the meeting before they walked into the meeting room. And there is no excuse for that.

So prepare for everything. Think what you are going to say, make sure it's a valuable contribution.

23

Burnt fingers

In the *scrambled up world of work* commitment does not come from a client's business affairs department in a brown enve-lope; it comes from mutual trust over an espresso or an email. So you can get your fingers burnt. And the main reasons are all about money:

! A client won't pay an invoice.

! A client will pay an invoice very late.

! You have to pay a supplier up front but you haven't got the money from the client yet and cash flow is going to be a struggle.

Whatever agreements or contracts you have in place with the client, it all comes down to *trust*. Whatever you have agreed/ signed on paper, unless you are going to take a client to court, at the end of the day it's about your relationship with the client and the mutual trust that will bond your agreement. And that's what will get an invoice paid. So make business decisions and enter into relationships on the basis of trust, not what it says on a bit of paper.

Some self-employed people I know always operate under signed contracts, job numbers and purchase orders for projects. I never bothered. Not because I was complacent but because that wasn't my style. Ironically, one of the only two clients where I ever had to use purchase orders queried the project and refused to pay.

When you are a one-person business unit it's difficult reconciling business development with debt chasing. One minute you're asking about the new project; the next you're pressuring to get an old invoice settled. And that can affect your relationship with the client.

Karen has a neat solution. Her mother looks after the money side. She provides a self-contained resource for financial management, and that's all she does for the business. Karen emails her mother job sheets and she turns these into invoices. Karen never has to worry about chasing payment; her mother – I mean, the accounts department – does all that for her. One plays good cop, the other bad cop.

Because in the *scrambled up world* you have to wear lots of hats, but being good cop and bad cop at the same time can be a bit too difficult.

24

Just like that

Not getting paid isn't the only downside to business with no rules. Without any rules to protect you, the risks of getting exposed are high. One of the reasons my marketing business was viable is that the offering was distinctive: offering clients a really unrivalled relationship in terms of intimacy, attention, availability and turnaround. But part of the appeal was that we didn't ask clients to sign contracts, letters of agreement or make long retainer-based commitments to us, because if we did then we knew we wouldn't get them as clients. If they had to do that they may as well go with the big guys.

The downside is that if clients want to quit, they can. A big client of mine called a meeting and announced they were ceasing to use us and taking the project in-house. 'When does this take effect from?' I asked.

'From now,' he replied.

'From now?' I queried.

'Yes.'

Gulp.

And our business changed. With no warning. Just like that.

And that's tough for a small enterprise, when a large part of your business goes out of the window. But of course that's the price to pay for the model we advocate.

The resulting effect on your business can be both scary and re-orienting. Looking at that blank canvas of a spreadsheet once again, scratching your head and asking, 'How I am going to replace all those lost revenues?' Of course I had absolutely no idea, but that's what I said *last time*, and then I got there in the end.

Just like that.

25

When to walk away

Don't be afraid of walking away from clients who prove trouble-some. Although flexibility is key, it's important to have some principles and if the client isn't adhering to them, then it may be time to move away. Examples of this could be:

! Clients who consistently want something for nothing.

! Clients who don't pay your invoices on time.

! Clients who want you to jump through hoops again and again and again when you have already proved your worth.

If the profit margin or kudos of association from that client is *so* significant, then stick with them. If not, quit.

It's not worth it.

Too many clients want too much for too little and it doesn't do any harm to stand your ground and – respectfully – say that it doesn't suit your commercial objectives to work that way. It never ceases to amaze me how many clients out there want you to do loads of work and not guarantee that they will pay you. They just don't get it.

I am a bit more old-fashioned: I like to provide a service and get paid for it.

26
Details

Make sure you get the details right.

In emails, documents, invoices. Lay them out right, make sure there are no mistakes.

When you are working for yourself, *everything* you produce is part of your offering, and a reflection of your brand. A poorly worded proposal or a shoddy-looking invoice will reflect badly. I got an invoice from a supplier. Sure, I'm not their most important client and they'd done me a great rate but they hadn't looked at the details. They'd overwritten an old template but not changed the address of the company. So it had my business name but with a completely different address. Not a huge problem, we all make mistakes, but it's worth checking the details.

I worked with a designer on a project. He's a creative, right? But his invoice was poorly written – it had been typed out in two minutes with no attention to layout. I make my invoices look professional and presentable – it takes no time to make a template or you can find one on the web.

You need to make sure all client-facing materials are present-able. It's a reflection of you – so get it right. Even the invoices.

Similarly, turn up and know who you are meeting. I had a meet-ing with a guy who turned up at the venue and said he was there to meet Chris. Not a great first impression. I got his name right. And whatever his talents I'll always remember him as the guy who got my name wrong. So do your research and do your prep. I was introduced to another guy who had just set up his own consultancy; we exchanged business cards. His card displayed the word 'Consutancy'. Not a good sign.

Also, pay attention to the details of your arrangement with the client. The deadline for a project, its parameters, your expecta-tions. And if the client has not confirmed the deal in writing about the deliverables, the timetable, the payment schedule, then do it yourself. Even if the client does send through con-firmations, do it yourself anyway and do it first. You'll get the reputation for being good at the details, which will hold you in good stead for the next deal/sale/project.

From confirmation to invoice, first meeting to project delivery, be consistent and make sure you are BIG on details.

27

Get it right online

Whatever you decide about the marketing tools you require, you'll need an online presence. Some small businesses still don't think they need websites. There are small, valid exceptions – companies with full order books and long lines of customers – but for most of us it's a must.

You might not need a bricks-and-mortar presence, but you do need an online one: a destination where you can sell your offering. Don't be fooled into thinking you need a flash, expensive, vast website – you just need a good basic one.

Don't underestimate your website – it's probably the first thing your client or target is going to see and first impressions count. Make sure you keep it simple:

- **!** Keep content to a minimum – 'less is more' applies here, so keep it focused and relevant. Focus on content that is not going to go out of date (unless you intend to update it regularly).

- **!** The look and feel should reflect your brand personality. If you have a distinctive market offering, don't have a mediocre website.

- **!** Think content over style, so go easy on animated welcome sequences that take ages to load (we're all bored of them).

- **!** Have a 'call to action' so there's the opportunity to use it as a sales driver and make sure it's easy for potential customers to get in touch.

So do it right. Especially if you are in creative services yourself. One design agency I was looking at had not updated their website since 2003 and that's what they do for a living! Another agency launched 12 months ago but still had 'website coming soon'. Not impressive.

You don't need big budgets, just a very clear idea of what you want to say. It should reflect your DNA; be the total sum of your offering to guide and inform all communications.

You've got to be a good self-publicist to succeed. If you're shy, forget it. Shout about what you do and how you do it, be prepared to email out, to pick up the phone and to be always thinking about promotional opportunities. Never miss a trick in the promotion of your business. Because promotion is the lifeblood of your business – it creates profile, interest, word of mouth and, ultimately, sales.

28

Don't hide from the customer

When you are a small business there is no excuse not to manage relationships properly. If your customer has a problem, then get on the phone to them instantly and communicate with them, deal with them right away.

It's easy to hide behind email when something goes wrong. And something *will* go wrong. Shit happens. Frequently. But don't cop out with an email and don't wait until a small problem becomes a big unmanageable problem. Call the client right away, apologize if there's a problem, say you're looking into it and that you'll report back. I had some technical problems on one of my projects. They were out of my hands; the supplier was way down the food chain, my supplier's supplier. But I did two things. I called up my client straight away to say we had a problem but we were dealing with it; and I kept on top of it until it was resolved. Because taking responsibility is a key part of customer service. It may not be your fault but it's your customer and it's your job to sort it out.

Because when you are building a business you cannot afford to get a bad reputation.

29

Getting regular gigs

Try to find a client or project that can give you a regular income each month because financial stability is not something you have a lot of when you work for yourself. A couple of regular monthly projects stripped across the year will give some foundation to a business plan that otherwise would be looking pretty damn empty, even if it's a few hundred quid a month.

When I first started working for myself I had regular consultancy commitments with plenty of clients who committed to at least four – and sometimes five – days a week. That was great but it didn't last forever. When they *Leap!* many people try to line up clients before they leave and some start out doing work for their former employer. But sometimes you just have to take that *Leap!* and work out where the clients are once you have stepped off that corporate treadmill. Because until you say you're available, you won't be able to drum up new business.

I may have started with solid regular commitments from clients but seven years later the reality is different. Multiple revenue streams, multiple disciplines, ups and downs, peaks and troughs.

It's a rollercoaster.

30

Bloody obvious management

My first business challenge as a young manager was an under-performing business unit that was given to me to evaluate and manage. The verdict? Why are we using so many hired-in free-lancers on jobs when staff are sitting around doing nothing?

It was so bloody obvious.

And it often is. But my predecessor had done nothing about it. Here's another. A sales manager in a culture that was so obsessed with systems and structures and reporting initiatives that she never actually did any selling herself. Four people in her team and she sat there like a spare part, doing nothing apart from printing off sales reports and acting as their report line.

Think of the result if she'd liberated herself from the paperwork and just got on and *sold*! Diagnosis: dump the over-bureaucratic systems and structures (this was a small business, not IBM). The results will speak for themselves, without the paperwork and reporting systems.

Coming up with solutions to your and your client's business are often so very easy. Don't overcomplicate things when you're diagnosing what's wrong. Business is rarely black or white, but sometimes it's as simple as something being right or wrong.

You'll be surprised at how often the obvious stuff gets overlooked by everyone else. Just make sure you don't make the same mistake with your own business.

31
Small is best

I'm a firm believer that 'small is best' when it comes to creativity of ideas and results: small units are great at devising effective and successful ideas. Get too big and you lose focus. And it's a fact that big business recognizes: many big corporations have leftfield satellite operations that act like start-ups in order to have the enterprise and innovation to stay progressive.

So don't think you need to embark on an expansion strategy to be successful: of course you need to build revenues and profits but you can retain a small team and a small client base to do so. Boutique operations are successful because they are small enough to give a personal level of attention, compact enough to ensure that personality pervades every part of the business and intimate enough to ensure they remain focused on what they're good at. Grow too big too quick and a company can lose what made it special in the first place.

I was introduced to a small business that produced radio commercials. The two partners had been running the company for five years and were now getting ambitious. They wanted to grow the operation into other areas: video production and studio hire. The partners didn't want to grow the activities one by one, they had their expansion plan and they wanted to put it in place now. But because they didn't have the team or resources to effectively deliver each new business strand, they ended up flirting with those new areas and took their eye off the ball of the core business. Clients were concerned the company weren't experts at making radio ads any more because the perception was that they had spread themselves too thin and into areas that made little sense to outsiders. A better strategy would have been to try one new area at a time, test it, get it right and then launch it, whilst ensuring the core business did not suffer. This company got it wrong by thinking too disparately.

Don't assume you need an organizational chart full of subsidiaries to be successful. Keep it small, focused and don't spread yourself too thin.

32
Get your hands dirty

Too many chiefs, not enough Indians. A problem in a lot of small, growing companies. A management team in place and not enough people actually *doing* the work. I've worked with a few small companies where this was a problem. One company had four members of staff. Three were appointed managers who did management and admin tasks but little in the actual task of production, of directly serving clients with a product. The one non-manager was the only one really sweating.

No one wanted to be hands-on; they thought they were above all that. The result was that the clients only saw the junior; he was the only visible one anyway and, ironically, he came to define the business, he was hands-on from sales to delivery.

Working for myself has taught me that clients like to work with me because it's *me* and that means you have to be hands-on. That can be tedious sometimes. For example, if a client wants you to account manage a project, you have to take care of everything including those all-important details. On one project I didn't check some copy in a brochure myself; and the client was frustrated at some 'schoolboy errors' that I would have spotted if I'd looked at it myself. It was frustrating but it reminded me why the client wanted me involved – because they knew I would check stuff myself.

Including the details.

So don't be shy of getting your hands dirty because you need to experience business at first hand. And being the boss doesn't necessarily mean you can stop doing the hands-on stuff, especially in a small business. Remember, you're always going to need more doers than managers.

33
Don't give too much away

When you're starting a business or courting a new client, inevitably you have to tease the client with something, give them some sense of your value through a taster of an idea, a proposal or whatever.

But don't give too much away.

As part of my proposal to a prospective client I produced a scope of works that detailed all the work I would be doing to launch a new venture. I knew it was giving away much of my intelligence but I had to demonstrate my know-how in the proposal *and* articulate the key stages in the project life cycle as well as show where their investment in me would go. By giving them this document before they committed, I gave them too much of my intelligence and expertise up front. They never did commission me to do the work, but by now had a blueprint of what they needed. It's a difficult one because I had little alternative.

Another time I was courting a big company for some consultancy work and produced a paper with some marketing ideas as a tease. This included the idea for a new marketing strapline for a new product launch. It was simple but effective and a few months later they introduced it with great success.

Someone in the company said it was a very simple idea and any-one could have thought of it. But they didn't. I did. I should have ensured its value was protected, quantified and better rewarded. But I never got paid for the idea itself. Make sure you only give away the teasers for free and quantify the big ideas, however simple, in order that the client learns to value your contribution.

34

Think 'entrepreneur', not 'freelance'

Whilst definitions are not as important as your attitude, you do need to be comfortable with how you describe yourself. When I went independent in 2000, some co-workers suggested I'd gone 'freelance'. Another, who was a good mentor to me, said I'd gone 'plural'.

Plural: yes, I liked that. But for me, never ever freelance. 'Free' maybe but independent, self-employed, running my own business is how I define myself professionally; freelance is dif-ferent.

Freelance is often working somewhere in a part-time role or on a contract basis, going into a client's workplace and working alongside a staff team, normally a single-discipline specialist. Sure, in the *scrambled up world* we do that some of the time but contract work is not always enterprising. Some industries rely on freelance or contract staff, such as the construction or television sectors. If you are a video editor or a camera operator, chances are you'll be freelance.

But the difference with *Leap!* is your attitude. It's about taking the next step. Not just hiring yourself out as an IT consultant or a camera operator, but taking it one stage further: the IT expert setting up an IT consultancy; the camera operator setting up a business booking crew and hiring equipment. 'Setting up a business' might only be you and your mate who you work with, but it's a different – more enterprising – philosophy. And that difference counts.

So, in the *scrambled up world* think entrepreneur, not freelance, because your attitude makes all the difference.

35
Avoid those faux pas

We can all say or do the wrong thing in front of clients. But when you work for yourself, you feel so much more account-able; faux-pas can be more embarrassing and also potentially damaging.

Early in my career I took a brief from the editor of *Travel Weekly* magazine. 'Is that a weekly or monthly publication?' I asked. It's that kind of brilliance that helps justify your fees.

One of my first assignments when I started working for myself was some consultancy work looking at the feasibility of a new venture in LA. I flew out there with a colleague who worked for the client. It was hard work, a lot of meetings squeezed into a couple of days. We started early and ended late. I was billing on a daily rate basis and because of the long hours, especially on travel days, the client had agreed to pay one and a half days' worth of fees per day for some of the trip.

One evening we had finished a meeting early and had a few minutes to kill before the next one. So we drove down to the coast and for five minutes took a stroll along the beach. My colleague Tony got his camera out and took some shots of the ocean, including one of me where I had taken my shoes off and was paddling in the water. The next week, back in London, I popped in to the client offices to give my invoice and expenses to the finance director. And there was Tony, showing his LA photos off: 'And there is Ian, down on the beach.' That photo looked like we were on holiday, taking the piss at the client's expense. Nice one, Tony.

Then there was the time I took an old-school client to a very new-school restaurant. When my client chose the beef the waiter said, 'The beef is served pink, sir,' at which point my client spluttered out his wine and I wished we'd gone to the local pub for dinner.

So, from choosing the right restaurant to insisting on a no-photograph rule on business trips, avoid those faux-pas.

36

Making a difference

A cliché. But a cliché worth heeding. In whatever you do, ask yourself this:

Did I make a difference?

With that proposal, with that service to a client, with that logo I designed, that website I produced, strategy I formulated, presentation I gave, photo I took, training day I ran, meeting I attended – did it make a difference?

If you strive to do this in all you do, it will give you that upper hand and clients/employers will choose you over mediocre and predictable alternatives that offer mediocre and predictable results. It's not always easy making a difference. It takes preparation, thought, effort. It takes innovation and insight. But it's the difference between being memorable and forgotten; distinctive and average; and ultimately, therefore, the difference between failure and success.

So, every time, *make a difference*.

If you don't – or worse, can't be bothered – you may as well forget trying to be a success.

Part Four
WORKLIFE

Now you have taken the *Leap!* to work for yourself, there is no going back. This is a very different kind of work to what you're used to do. It's not 9–5, or even 8–7, because it's harder to define.

It's a very *different* kind of working life, where the rules fly out of the window. You have a great deal of flexibility but also an enormous responsibility. The good news is that working for yourself means you can take a break on a summer's day when all your friends are stuck in their offices. But it also means dealing with a client or writing a proposal when you're meant to be on holiday.

And there's a whole load of other challenges: working from home, staying motivated, how you reconcile that 'work/life balance', whatever that is.

But remember this is a real positive move for you – you are in control of all you do and that is a great, liberating feeling.

Success is not just about your pay packet any more (there is no 'pay packet'), it's much more complex than that. It's about defining the new 'you' but, most of all, it's just about one word:

SURVIVAL.

1

If you don't want to know the score, look away now

Let's get the bad news out of the way now.

It's going to be tough at times.
You'll get lonely.
Cash flow can be difficult.
Getting sales is not easy.
OK?

So what's going to make it easier?

! A support network of co-workers and mentors.

! A positive outlook.

! Friends and family who understand this is different, and offer support and encouragement.

! Clients and the promise of work.

! A financial safety net for those lean months.

! A physical – and dedicated – workspace (not the corner of your bedroom).

What's the journey like?

It's like what I heard on the radio this morning in the bathroom: a lone round-the-world yachtsman talking about his current voyage. 'What's been the best thing about the trip?' he was asked. 'Freedom,' I mumbled to the mirror as I shaved. 'Freedom,' replied the yachtsman. 'And the worst?'

'When you are in a gale and being blown against the rocks,' came the response.

And that's what it's like in the *scrambled up world of work*.

2

It's a life thing

For many who have taken the *Leap!* it's about something very simple:

Being in control.

More and more we want to take control of our lives: from designing our own homes to growing our own vegetables, we all want to be in control. So it's no surprise that people take the *Leap!* to be in control of their own destiny, to shape what they do, how they do it and where they do it from.

It may sound clichéd but when you start working for yourself you really can shape and create your own destiny. You need to ensure you make the necessary investment of ideas, enthusiasm and talent in order to create a success. It's a direct result of what you put in.

But when your business existence is threatened or exposed, it's not just your business at stake, it's your whole being. Kathryn took the *Leap!* a few weeks ago and it's all been going well. But she got a legal letter the other day – from her former employer, warning her not to proceed with a new area of business because it breached a non-compete clause in her old employment contract. To Kathryn, this isn't just an obstacle to one area of her business; this could effectively threaten her whole existence. Because when you start working for yourself the relationship between your personal and business self is very intimate, it's intricately linked. There is no separation as you might have had in your old job, you can't just say, 'Oh well, that's a work thing,' because business becomes a life thing.

When you hit problems, challenges or obstacles it may threaten your whole well-being. You are your business and that means you can't help taking knocks personally.

So you just have to focus on what you *can* control to resolve the problems. Being in control is such a positive force: if you control your working life, your working day, you can make a choice. A choice about how hard you work. A choice about juggling work with childcare; juggling worktime with playtime. If you start work at 07.00, you can choose to finish early. That type of flexibility is difficult if you work for someone else because it's out of your control.

My father's generation went off to work in the morning and came back in the evening. Work was pretty much separate from home life. In the *scrambled up world of work* it's all mixed up.

For those of us who spend much of the week working at home there is not that traditional separation. You may be visible to wives, husbands, partners, flatmates, kids during the day. Which is good and bad. Bad because they might distract work; good because that's one of the benefits of working for yourself and choosing when and where to work. OK, in the old days Daddy was not sitting at his desk at 11 p.m. or checking his emails on a Saturday morning but Daddy probably didn't see his two-year-old son Monday to Friday either. So you take the rough with the smooth – you get to see more of your family during the working day; they may get to see less of you during weekends and evenings.

When I was a small boy I struggled to understand the concept of work. I thought workers like my father were given instructions at the train station each morning for what they had to do once they got to the office. I didn't understand self-enterprise, autonomy or responsibility. I never could have imagined how things change and that no one except yourself tells you what to do. That there is that freedom to manage your own time. Adjusting to that is an important discipline; you have to ask yourself if it's OK taking a day off for your birthday; the holiday request forms go in your own in-tray.

That's a lot of responsibility but at least you get to make the decisions.

3
Nostalgia trips

Let's get nostalgic.

What do I miss?

! I miss having a long lunch with colleagues on a Friday, on someone else's time and at someone else's expense. I miss that camaraderie of a bunch of people out together with lots in common and a real bond.

! I miss being able to delegate when I go on holiday and being able to switch off.

! (Because I work from home a lot) I miss the fact that coming in the front door is not about the end of the working day, it's more about walking up to my office and having a stack of work to do.

! I miss knowing what I am earning month in, month out.

! I miss paid holidays and expense claims.

! I miss stability.

What don't I miss?

! Travelling on the tube in rush hour, commuting every day.

! Not being able to make a single-handed decision and lots of them quickly.

! Company politics and administration.

! Doing stuff I don't agree with.

! Arguing for a pay rise.

! Having to tolerate colleagues who don't pull their weight.

! All that corporate 'clutter' that gets in the way of actually doing the business.

4

Do you love stress?

Is life in the *scrambled up world of work* stressful?

You bet.

My mortgage goes out of my account on the 16th, so my first question concerns how much I am earning this month. What's my turnover looking like? What are my projected costs? Some months, cash flow will be bad and you'll ask yourself these questions again and again.

Not meeting your boss's quarterly sales targets is one thing; not making enough sales when you are on your own is another. Because the buck stops with you, the responsibility for bringing in the revenues lies only with you. And if you can't meet your outgoings or sustain the cash flow you'll have an additional pressure and one that threatens all of us in the *scrambled up world of work*: can you make enough money? Enough to pay the bills? To pay for the business overhead you require to operate? All that personal overhead for you and your family?

That's a lot of question marks.

And doing all those things you have to do whilst struggling to spin all those plates and having no one to help. If you're a one-man band, there's no one to cover you when you are away, no one to delegate to when you are off sick. That will get stressful too.

5

A space to work

Where you work is important. You need a dedicated workspace somewhere. In your spare room at home, in a serviced office, in a shed at the bottom of the garden, in a coffee shop. But make sure there is a *separation* between where you relax and where you work. If you choose to work at home don't try to work in the corner of your bedroom or living room – you'll find it impossible to switch off. Because it's hard enough blurring work and play as it is, so you have to make sure you can shut the door of the office. So wherever you choose to work, it's got to have a door.

For homeworkers, when work threatens to take over your house, shut the paperwork behind that door. You need to introduce some physical parameters between workspace and playspace.

If you have a partner or family and you work at home, have some rules. If the door is shut it means you are not to be disturbed; each party should act as if the other is not there. When I work at home, my wife is often there, working herself or looking after our son. But we communicate via an internal phone and email; we may only be two floors away but we need to act as if we're in different places. And that helps delineate between work and family.

There is a new trend for garden offices. In fact 'shedworking' is not new; writers and artists have worked in sheds and summerhouses for generations. The bonus of a garden workspace is that there is a separation between where you live and where you work and with WiFi you don't even need an extra broadband connection. Salim is a radio producer who has built an office space and edit suite at the end of his garden, away from his noisy kids; Sam is another shedworker who runs a small record label from an outbuilding at the back of her garden.

Of course there are plenty of small businesses where you might need a showroom, client-friendly offices or a small manufacturing capability and you might need a 'proper' office for that. If not, a home can be one of the most effective places to at least start a business, not least because you don't have to pay for it.

6

Somewhere else

If you spend most of your time in your job sitting at your desk, it's easy to forget you aren't going to have the best ideas sitting there.

Ten years ago, a talented radio producer asked his boss if he could go and sit by a lake to think up new programme ideas. He was visionary enough to know he would not come up with 'The Big Idea' at his desk. But maybe he was naïve enough to think his boss would say yes. His boss – of course – laughed at him. The producer went back to his desk. But later he quit his job and went on to enjoy much success elsewhere, where he found the freedom to search for that big idea.

If you are going to be creative you aren't going to get any results sitting at your desk. But you might not get taken seriously if you ask to go and sit by the lake. Maybe just do it anyway?

Whether a lakeside or a coffee shop, make sure you liberate yourself from your desk and go somewhere else. Just getting out and changing your space does so much.

7

Motivation

Yeah, I admit it. It's tough getting motivated sometimes.

Especially when you are only answerable to yourself and you may not have any co-workers to hassle you or support you, to say, 'Where's that report?' or 'Did you email Samira back?' And if you work from home, it can be even harder to get going.

Procrastination is the potential downfall of every *Leap!* entrepreneur. So you have to be disciplined. My discipline is in managing my tasks by having a daily 'to-do' list. And if I don't get everything done that day, then I have to transfer the tasks to the next one, when it's already full of tasks. That pressure motivates me to get things done.

Being answerable to yourself might sound well and good but on a rainy Monday morning when you are working at home, don't have any meetings to go to and wish you were back in bed, it can be hard work to get motivated.

Because no one will bat an eyelid if you decide to 'cancel' the day and do something else instead.

No one, that is, apart from you.

The day might stretch ahead of you like a huge blank canvas. That and a bulging to-do list of all those people to target, those invoices to do and that research to get underway. And it takes stacks of self-discipline and self-sufficiency to stay motivated and get on with it.

You have to give shape and purpose to your working day. You have an opportunity. A blank canvas on which to create something, a blank sheet of paper. And that should feel good.

But we all have days when it's difficult to get started. Inevitably you are going to get stale.

Stale in how, when and where you work. Bogged down with some administration, stuck with a tedious project. And when that happens you need to let in some fresh air to change the routine:

! Take time out.

! Go out for lunch with a friend or mentor.

! Switch the model.

! Change the position of your desk; reinvigorate your workspace.

! Have a makeover – go and get your hair done.

Any change can be so effective, however small.

On those days when I get stale I know I need to do something. Walk out of the room, walk around the block, go and have a coffee, go somewhere else.

And two things will happen:

1   You will feel liberated.

2   You'll return to your desk with a fresh perspective and clarity about all you have to do.

They say a week away has restorative powers. Well, never underestimate the power of one *hour* away.

Get stimulated

The reality is that many of those eureka moments I've had in business have been aided by stimulation of one kind or another:

! That single espresso (or was it a double?).

! That can of Red Bull.

! The First Beer Of The Day.

They have kick-started my brain into action and been a real stimulus, giving me the clarity to find the solution, the idea, the strategy, whatever.

I should also give credit to those other stimulants that have helped me in business:

! Fresh air.

! Journeys.

! Stunning vistas.

! Sunshine.

! Lying on a sunbed by a pool.

I do all my best thinking on planes and trains.* Getting on a train is not a disruption to the working day; it's a platform (excuse the pun) for stimulation. Away from my desk with ever-changing scenery, I get my best ideas.

So go take a journey. Somewhere. Anywhere.

---

* This chapter was written on the 18.05 Leeds to Kings Cross train.

9
Benchmarks that really count

In the old economy, success was all about being 'Head of Sales' or 'Brand Manager'; it was about what it said on your business card, what status you had. But in the *scrambled up world of work*, it's about a different set of benchmarks.

Measuring success is no longer about those traditional corporate benchmarks. It's less about where you are on the corporate ladder, what position you occupy, what your perceived status is, even what your earnings are.

Instead, success is more about such intangibles as freedom, happiness and emancipation, and you can't measure them.

And, more importantly, you might measure your success by something much simpler: SURVIVAL. That you survived the first six months or even six years of going it alone is worth a celebration. That you are still here. That you have some great projects under your belt. That you have some happy clients. That you've managed to generate £0.5 million in sales to date. Or something less financial: that you managed to make your kids' sports day this year.

But the bottom line does count in this world too because if you aren't making enough, then freedom, happiness and emancipation go out of the window.

So many business success stories are about companies growing big, it's easy to think you have to grow big to be successful. But big is not always better. Smaller businesses can be more effective, more creative and more successful.

One guy I know is always asking me when I am going to get a 'proper' office and hire some 'proper' staff, as if these are the only benchmarks for success. But because I don't have staff and premises to worry about, I can be more enterprising. I prefer to benchmark using different criteria, not whether I have bricks-and-mortar walls and staff on a payroll. Instead:

! In the last 12 months did I make a difference to the project, to the client?

! Did I stretch myself, did I learn stuff?

! Did I enjoy myself?

! Did I make some money? Was it enough?

! Did I achieve something significant, did I bring something to fruition, create something from nothing?

! Did I have the right balance of leisure time vs work time? Did I have enough flexibility to enjoy myself, go on holidays, play with my son, go for that run, and go to that art gallery?

To do all those things that I wouldn't be able to do in 'proper' jobs?

And that's all that counts.

The flexibility I have had has been fantastic. When I work from home I've been able to spend special time with my young son, seeing him growing up at close quarters. If I had that 'proper' job, I'd rarely see him Monday to Friday as he'd be asleep when I'd get home.

And that experience, despite all the developments in my business, is priceless.

10

A secret

I'm going to let you into a secret.

When you do your own thing and work for yourself, you can do *anything*!

I saw an old schoolfriend the other day. We hadn't seen each other for 20 years. He's a commodity trader in the City. He's good at his job. But then it struck me: this guy has been a trader, sitting in a similar environment, working in the same sector, day in, day out, for 20 years. And that's why he's good. And he may have another 12 years doing it. That's what specialists do. The Same Thing. Whereas in my 20 years at work, I have done a range of projects and assignments – such variety which has challenged and stimulated me.

I know this is not the exception – lots of people do the same thing, in the same environment and using the same tools for years and years. It's what my father's generation did. And, indeed, it's what a lot of self-employed do too. I know:

! Good designers.

! Great writers.

! Really good brand managers.

! Genius copywriters.

! PR experts.

People who are great at *one* thing.

And when you work for an employer that's why they hire you. But in the self-employed world you can make a living by doing a whole range of 'stuff':

! I'm writing this book.

! I have just written a report for a client formulating ideas on how they can grow their business.

! I'm managing and producing marketing campaigns.

- *!* I'm advising an arts festival on promotion.

- *!* I'm copywriting a sales document for a media client.

- *!* I'm advising a small financial-services business on marketing.

- *!* I'm involved in a new media-training venture.

- *!* I've co-devised a new children's intellectual property.

That is what I am up to, just this month – in the space of a week or two, literally. I can't think of anyone I know with such an eclectic mix. And I can't think of any single business doing all this and 'getting away' with such variety.

But you can do what you want to do. How amazing is that?

So be prepared to rewrite the rulebook. Single expertise may be the convention of business success; *multi-discipline success* is much harder, but if you can pull off that variety, the rewards are really worth it and, more importantly, you can make sure you never do the same thing again.

11

There is always an alternative

Sometimes, try liberating yourself from the to-do list to start your day differently. Rather than starting your working week knee-deep in emails with a long list of tasks ahead of you, do something different. One recent Monday morning I started the week with a run. It was a refreshing way to start the day and something I would never normally do, especially on a Monday. It felt good. Good to have a change.

And as I ran across the footbridge over the railway I looked down at all the commuters boarding their train to the City. They didn't look too happy; some of them clearly had the 'Monday morning feeling'. I felt like I'd discovered a secret of an alternative lifestyle; it's as if they weren't aware that they didn't *have* to take the commuter option. I wanted to shout, 'There *is* an alternative.'

Having the flexibility to manage your own workload is a real benefit when you work for yourself. Ishali runs her own marketing business. She works hard, she works long days. But every Monday morning she goes to the gym for a session with her personal trainer. That's how she starts her week and who says she can't? When you work for yourself it's easier to time-shift your work commitments to accommodate the nice stuff, to take a break and go and play some tennis or to browse in a bookshop. And you can be certain that you'll be making up the time later, because when you work for yourself there's no such thing as 'skiving off'.

Self-employed friends of mine disappear to the golf course some mornings, just because they can. The other morning, as I was having breakfast with my wife and son, my wife said, 'Let's go to the zoo today.'

'Don't be silly – I haven't got time to go the zoo, I've got stacks of work to do,' I said.

'What's the point of working for yourself if you can't go to the zoo once in a while?' came her response.

And she – kind of – had a point. And since I had no meetings that day I could conceivably go out for a few hours. So I knuckled down to a morning of calls and tasks, and we went out in the afternoon to the zoo.

So make the most of your flexibility and take that trip to the zoo. Because you don't have to ask anyone's permission when you work for yourself.

12

A love of speed

I overheard this comment the other day:

> 'He was quite new at the company; he'd only been there
> three years.'

I nearly fell off my chair. In the *scrambled up world of work*,
business moves so quickly, and 'new' is much more current
than that. Rates of change are far more radical and dramatic
than ever. Three years is not new.

Things happen fast when you work for yourself. From an idea
on the train to putting it into practice is now a matter of minutes
or hours rather than weeks or months.

And that speed has an enormous impact on what you can
achieve when you work for yourself. Making decisions becomes
so much more efficient. You don't have to fill in any forms; you
don't need to formulate a proposal; it doesn't need to go to a
board meeting; it doesn't need authorizing by a boss in a different time zone in Atlanta.

I had lunch with a client the other day, a big business. Richard
heads up a division and he was waiting for his boss to approve

some figures, some financial projections. It was May. How long had his boss had them to approve? Since December …

When you're working for yourself you can make quick decisions. Executives who sit on decisions for months will ultimately make themselves extinct.

So you can't afford not to be fast.

13
From feast to famine

When you work for yourself it's difficult to know when the work's going to flow. And you can't pick and choose what you do when. If you could spread 12 months' work across the year in equal workloads that would be great, but the market is much more scrambled than that. So, some months you're going to be frantic, and in others you'll be quiet. You'll have to grab opportunities when and where you can.

Some weeks you need to be prepared to work evenings and weekends to keep up with the workflow, in others you might have the flexibility to take it easy, or take it easier.

Some breaks and holidays will come at a good time, when you can take a break. Others will come at a bad time when you just won a piece of new business and have to spend the second day of your holiday driving around rural Spain in search of a WiFi connection or Internet café.

So it can be either feast or famine in the *scrambled up world of work*. And there's not much you can do about that.

So manage your expectations accordingly.

14

What is 'the working day'?

In our BlackBerry-equipped, *always-on* culture, the concept of a working day with strict parameters is outdated. We work when we need to, responding to and dealing with clients not just during the weekday but also at evenings, weekends, whenever. One reason a client liked our relationship was that he knew I was available at weekends and in the evenings and I took the judgement that their business was important enough to merit me providing that level of service. If I was only available 9–5, I would have lost the business.

One weekend I had problems with my WiFi network. I'd just moved house so didn't have a local IT guy that I could call upon. I found a website of a local company that looked like they could help so I dispatched an email to an 'info@' address. It was a Sunday afternoon. A guy emailed back to me that evening.

My wife said, 'That was quick ... on a Sunday.'

And she was right. But I take it for granted that when you run a micro-business, you have to be on the case 24/7. And to be successful, you have to be quick. Even on a Sunday.

Even for the more traditional roles, the line between work and play is blurring. I met a corporate bank manager recently. She doesn't have a 'proper' office, and is either based at home or is out visiting clients, with a virtual PA at head office 20 miles away. She likes the flexibility that brings: working in the early hours and late at night, and then going swimming at a health club each morning for a couple of hours. I bet that's where she has the best ideas.

Friends of mine who see me sitting in a café say, 'Not working today?' Just because I'm not in an office doesn't mean I'm not working. I am, of course, always working. And if I'm in a café looking into thin air, I'm probably doing the really serious stuff:

THINKING.

15

Budgets, business plans and babies

Although things should be better in the 21st century, women still suffer from sexism in the traditional workplace. A few years back a (male) contact of mine commented on the high proportion of women working at my old company. He said, 'That's a lot of secretaries.' Except he wasn't joking. Another time, a consultant was doing some work on a project and he said, 'Perhaps one of the girls can get the teas in', when most of the women present were senior to the blokes. Thankfully business and society has changed, although not as much as it should have.

In the self-employed world, it's more of a meritocracy and gender is less of an obstacle; there's no glass ceiling. Accordingly women have found that they can better pursue their entrepreneurial dreams working for themselves. Working mothers become so adept at multi-tasking that they can be so much better at doing loads of stuff at once. The lifestyle and flexibility of work-at-home entrepreneurs also suits many women returning to work after having a baby.

For young mothers, life as a *Kitchen Table Entrepreneur* can be an appealing option, offering a low-risk way of starting a business or re-entering the workplace. It's the perfect test bed for your business skills to try an idea out, and pregnancy and maternity are often a great gestation for innovative business ideas. So many successful women have started businesses like this, conceiving ideas whilst they're pregnant that they develop months later.

And new business ventures are a bit like babies: that newfound sense of commitment and responsibility, those sleepless nights and, most controversial of all, what on earth are we going to call it??

Now that will really keep you up all night.

16

Trying to switch off

Taking holidays can be difficult because it's tough taking time off when there's no one to delegate to.

And it's not just frustrating when you want to take time off to lie on a beach – the same applies for taking time off for maternity or paternity leave. When my first son was born, a friend of mine in a traditional job said, 'Paternity leave is great – you catch up on all those things you have been meaning to do, like sort out your car insurance.' He didn't understand how different it was if you work for yourself.

Sure, I would be taking some time out but no one was paying me for it. I certainly wasn't spending it sorting out car insurance. Indeed, the month my son was born was one of my busiest in recent years, so there was a lot to do in those days after the birth and no one to delegate to. And that meant taking calls from clients even the day after, when I was at the hospital with my wife.

I went to see my acupuncturist the other day and as I lay there on the couch in my underwear she said, 'Ian, you look like you're at a meeting.' And that would have been an odd way to dress for a meeting but I had my arms folded and I guess I looked kind of tense. And, to me, the acupuncture session was like a meeting; it was sandwiched in the middle of my working day. It had a start time and an end time, and I had put it in my schedule as I would a business appointment. And as she put on the soothing music and asked me to relax, all I could think about was the 17 things I needed to do as soon as I turned my phone back on and got back to my desk.

Which reminded me of the price I pay for my 'freedom' in the *scrambled up world of work*: I am crap at switching off. Knowing your weakness is half the challenge; I now make more effort to relax at weekends and on holidays.

17

Home time ...

If you work at home you won't waste time on a daily commute because your workplace is a flight of stairs, not a train ride, away. So you can be more efficient with your time. But the downside is that you won't have 'me time', no time to unwind between work and play. Commuting may be a bore but at least that journey on the train, in the car or walk along the street gives you a chance to reflect, sleep or daydream. It's also a punctuation mark. It's a fresh page in your day as you end the 'work' bit and start the 'home' bit. The journey represents something very significant: a gear change.

You leave work, your brain full of what you did, what you didn't do, who said what. The journey home allows you to take stock, read that report, make those notes. And when your key goes in your front door, a sigh of relief.

Home.

You kick off your shoes, open that bottle of wine and switch on the TV. But working for yourself and working from home is a radically different experience. And that means the transition from working day to dinner can often be seamless. And that's harder.

No train ride for you to look out the window, to reflect on the day and to start relaxing, switching off. There is no buffer there. So you have to look at creating one – going for a run or even walk around the block at the end of the working day to create the buffer, to help you wind down.

Otherwise work and home will blur into one – so create a wind-down zone.

18

Taking time out

So if one thing is clear, it's that the line between work and play is not all clear. In fact it's a real blur. That's good and bad. Because, for the true entrepreneur, you never stop thinking about business ideas.

Sitting on a balcony under a moonlit sky on holiday, I'm still thinking about business stuff. And there's no easy switch-off. Work = life; you can't switch modes. It's what comes naturally; it's what I am. Sitting in a quiet moment and *not* thinking about business or my latest project is a rarity. In such a moment – on holiday – I thought of writing this very book. During another holiday – seven months later – I'm finishing this book.

This attitude is just an extension of your personality and it's an essential attribute in any entrepreneur or *wantrepreneur's* tool kit.

If all your best ideas are on weekends, in down time, on holiday, then you need to take a lot of holidays and/or go on lots of journeys/trips. We're called 'Mr and Mrs Holiday' by some friends but they don't realize that a holiday or trip away every two months is my prescription for great ideas. It's the necessary top-up to keep me stimulated, fresh and buzzing.

So remember to keep taking time out so you can make sure you are getting all the stimulation you need.

Of course it's tough – on you and your family – that every holiday involves you, a drink and a notepad, constantly churning out the next idea.

If regular trips and holidays are impractical, then think about taking time out during the working day.

A friend has just taken a senior job with an advertising agency. This agency is progressive in its outlook and realizes that you are not going to have creative ideas sitting at your desk. So he's been told that he has to prove that at least 15% of his working week must be doing 'nothing', getting out of the office and just thinking. Thinking and brainstorming new ideas, new projects.

We always put meetings in our diaries and organizers. But what about the really important thinking time – that 15%? Go through your diary and allocate 15% of the week as thinking time. Block it out as if it's a meeting. Prepare for it as if it's a meeting and then use the time to have some great ideas. If you're really busy this week, use the time on the train or at lunch. But liberate yourself from the iPod or the newspaper and do some thinking.

And if you can't do 15%, do 10% or 5%.

19

No rungs on the ladder

When you work in a proper job you get promoted. And it's all quite predictable.

Sales executive to sales manager; features writer to editor. You climb those rungs of the ladder.

But in the *scrambled up world of work* there are no rungs. You appointed yourself as top dog on day one when you set up your business and there's no going up from there. As your business gets more successful, so do you. Sure, you'll learn more, do more and become more proficient at a load of stuff, but there's no journey of ascendancy for you to embark on.

It's much flatter when you work for yourself. You run your own business. That's it. And that makes progress more difficult to quantify because you don't have a traditional career path you can track.

No fancy job titles, no sliding pay sale. No mapped out career route. There's no boss to impress, no new job to fight over. Success and progression are measured by what you achieved today, not by your annual appraisal.

20

Who wanted a job for life anyway?

There are still – in some industries – such things as a 'job for life'. Life in the *scrambled up world of work* is anathema of such a principle, it's about creating and building your own set of jobs. Of creating your own destiny and not being a slave to someone else's.

Our parents' generation was a world of jobs for life or of long spells in the same job, in 10- or 20-year blocks.

The notion of working for one employer for so long scares me – that kind of commitment locked in a single culture seems unhealthy. If a corporate environment could afford me the same level of autonomy, reward, diversity and enterprise that I currently enjoy then I'd be tempted, but a job or an environment 'for life' that's not going to change much – that sounds more like a life sentence.

Lisa is a partner in her own dental practice. I asked her if she might move some place else. No way, she has her practice and her client base – that's it now. She wouldn't dream of moving to another town, away from her clients. Bill is an accountant and a partner in a small firm. He's 34. 'What's next for you?' I asked.

'I'm a partner in the firm,' he said, 'so I'm not going anywhere now. This is me until retirement.'

Yes, these are talented people, in their own business partnerships, but because they're not doing it solo, they're locked into long-term arrangements with others. There'll be changes along the way but no radical reinvention. Me? I'll go for radical reinvention please.

21

The importance of self-sufficiency

There are lots of things I take for granted.

One is my self-sufficiency.

I have to do everything (no choice):

! Invoicing.

! Winning business.

! Arranging meetings.

*! Writing proposals.

*! Doing budgets.

*! Writing reports.

*! Delivering business.

If you are a one-person business unit, you are going to miss the joy of delegation. Delegating that bit of research you didn't want to do, that sales call you definitely didn't want to make, even that trip to the stationery store. Not only is delegation an efficient way of spreading the workload and optimizing skill sets, but also, to the business leader, it's a way of not having to do the boring stuff any more.

Sure, you can outsource some stuff, but in the *scrambled up world of work* you often have to do everything, the stuff you like and the stuff you don't. And unfortunately there is no choice; you *have* to do everything because no one else will do it for you.

You need to apply the same philosophy and approach to all the tasks you do, including the stuff you don't like. Being professional, tenacious, committed to the big and the small stuff, because it's all equally important.

I heard about a guy the other day who is quite senior in his industry. He'd spent a lot of his career working for a big organization and he'd got used to the support, the safety net.

But there are no safety nets once you've taken the *Leap!*. And now he has gone independent, he's struggling. He can't do the basics by himself. He's not good at setting up meetings, he's not good at following them up, he's not good at doing all the admin. Underneath the surface he's a great talent but unless he replicates that support he had in the big corporation, he's not worth so much to clients.

Life outside organizations is good because you are in control, but there is no one to take care of you and your family apart from you. In the old economy you gave yourself to an organization for your working life and they looked after you and your family. But you can forget all that now.

Self-sufficiency is a necessity. And if you can't hack it alone, maybe you should stay in the 'proper job'.

22

Where is everybody?

I heard an interview with a singer–songwriter. The journalist asked him what it had been like writing his debut album. He replied that it had been tough; it was just about him, no one to help him and no infrastructure to support him. He had to find the energy and creativity on his own to deliver the album. And that's what it can feel like when it's just you on your own.

Once you go it alone it's no surprise to learn it's going to get lonely. Missing water-cooler moments, discussing last night's *Apprentice* with colleagues, missing that sense of belonging.

Because whatever the merits of life in the *scrambled up world of work*, you might miss being part of an organization. Being part of a bigger picture.

And you shouldn't underestimate the social side of work. When I was single, living alone and working hard, work *was* my social life. Drinking and eating with clients, suppliers, colleagues.

I joked that when I quit work to do my own thing I tried Internet dating as most of my girlfriends had been through work (except I wasn't joking).

I used to like the office Christmas party. When you work for yourself, the office party can be a solitary occasion – so one year I invited other people I knew who worked for themselves; the next year a friend organized something similar for about 12 of us. Then, as my virtual team grew, I invited everyone who worked with me over the year to the Christmas lunch and it didn't seem so lonely.

Whether Christmas lunch or Facebook networks, you'll need to come up with some ideas to stop you getting lonely.

23
Making it up as you go along

I like breaking the rules, or rather having no rules; not just because it suits me personally, but in an ever-changing market-place, I think this is the *only* way to survive.

I was talking to a friend about her nephew. He's 16 but doesn't know what he wants to do when he leaves school. When I was his age I had clear ambitions but now, 20 years later, I am not sure *exactly* what I want to do, which is why I am working for myself. I do what I want, I make it up as I go along and if I want to change tack (just like that), no one's stopping me.

Business success stories will often talk about grand plans or strategies that got them where they are today. But for a lot of us, in an ever-changing marketplace, it's actually about making it up as you go along.

You just have to be honest enough to admit it.

24

Getting a return

Sometimes you'll have tough days, when you feel lethargic and lack motivation. You'll feel stale but you have no co-workers you can talk to, no boss to ask for guidance and direction.

And it's challenging because you have to find the answers within to search for direction or focus: it's all down to you. After all, that's what self-sufficiency is all about. But it's amazing how the little things can inspire and provide that focus. The other week I had a bad Monday, couldn't knuckle down, couldn't get started. And then in the shower on Tuesday I had *that* clarity, that focus and direction. I came out, grabbed a notepad and quickly emptied my brain of all those action points and ideas.

And my week got better.

Once the revenues start coming in, it gets really rewarding. Sending that invoice, seeing the money hit your account. And when you finally have the opportunity to take some time out and head off on holiday, it's very rewarding to realize that *you* got yourself here. No one else did. You didn't rely on a pay cheque, on your chief executive or your manager, on that corporation you used to work for to pay for those nice things in life. You have done it all yourself. *You are self-sufficient!* And that sense of self-sufficiency is very satisfying. It feels very liberating – it's the raw basics of commerce. You provide a trade and you get paid for it. And that's how the world goes round. And that feels good – every time you send an invoice and every time you bank a cheque. It's a great sense of achievement.

And then you realize it's *all* worth it.

25

What you do, not where you are

I'm writing this bit sitting in a room in London WC2. In the corner is a bar. There's soft music playing. Around the room are sofas, armchairs and coffee tables. I can count 11 laptops fired up, people sitting in clusters, others alone. People are talking, typing away. Some have a coffee in front of them; another has a beer. They are aged 25–45, dressed casually in jeans, T-shirts and jumpers.

Five years ago this scene would undoubtedly be described as 'Play'. But today it's 'Work'. These people are working. They are all entrepreneurs, most of them working for themselves or small businesses. It may look like play but this is serious stuff!

They're having meetings, doing deals, taking project briefs, brainstorming solutions, coming up with The Big Idea. Lots of raw talent outside the corporate infrastructure.

On the way out of this scene I walked past a building that houses a finance company. The blinds were open and I could see people at their desks in an open plan office, on the phone, typing at their keyboards. A very traditional office environment. But a world away from us *scrambled up* entrepreneurs.

But whether traditional workspace or a funky bar, remember that *work isn't a room with four walls; it's an attitude, it's what you do*, not *where you are.*

26

Giving up

A few years back, I had a bad year, but I didn't give up. I kept going. And I am so glad I did.

Because if I'd quit then and gone back to the job market, I would have been in a poor position. A self-employed professional with an under-performing business wanting a senior position. Would you hire me? An entrepreneur running a business that had seen good and bad times but survived; now that's an asset. You have to go through the bad times to appreciate the good.

I remember that year when I went to my accountant and he looked at my monthly figures. 'You took a holiday in February?' he asked. I hadn't but there was a hole in my revenues. I'd billed nothing. Zero.

I've enough experience now to know that holes happen, to look at three months or 12 months is a better indicator than a monthly snapshot of your financial health, so take the long view and don't panic.

Six consecutive bad months? Then something is wrong.

One or two bad months? Shit happens.

So persevere, don't beat yourself up, sit back and reflect before you make a big decision like quitting.

27

Is there any going back?

Once you've taken the *Leap!* to *the scrambled up world of work*, is there any going back?

Talking to my self-employed network, the only reason they say they'd go back to a proper job is if they really needed the financial security for their mortgage or their family. So if you can achieve that financial security when you go it alone, you don't need to ever go back.

And the longer you are in control, the more difficult it is to lose that, to go back to report to someone else, to live by an employer's rules. To lose that autonomy, that flexibility, that free spirit. And add all that up and it's a hell of a lot to lose.

I was offered a job by a big American company. I liked the sound of the role and they offered me a good package but I didn't like the rigidity of their working practices. You *will* be in the office by 8.15; you *won't* leave until 7 p.m. I am not shy of hard work, but on my own rules. Working from home was also not part of the culture. With the job out of town and at least an hour's commute by car via a route notorious for congestion, I turned the job down because it didn't fit in with my lifestyle. They offered to throw more money at me, but it wasn't about the money.

On the one hand, a *Leap!* entrepreneur is very valuable to an employer as an enterprising manager; on the other, you have become so independent, you could almost be unemployable! To conform goes against the grain of life in the *scrambled up world*. We revel in being different, not fitting in with organizational culture. We are masters at doing things our way, not their way.

28

A new way of being

Once you have entered the *scrambled up world of work* and are working for yourself, you'll have a whole new approach to life and work.

I met up with an old colleague who works for a medium-sized business. He's stuck in a rut, missing the exciting stuff of business.

Missing doing the deal, winning business, the adrenalin and risk of it all. And whilst there are hundreds of opportunities out there where he can find what he's missing working for others, there is one place where he can rediscover all this – working for himself.

If you pull it off, working for yourself can give you a whole load of benefits in how you run your life.

Yes, it's stressful but it gives you an opportunity no employer can provide: the opportunity to do your own thing; to write your own job description; to be responsible for everything from sales to accounts; to be a small – but perfectly formed – self-sufficient entrepreneur.

That experience gives you self-belief, confidence and a sense of achievement that is so basic. That with your raw materials (those ideas and that contact book) you *did* make something out of nothing; you created a product that clients wanted to buy; you billed them and, what's more, they paid you.

You don't answer to someone else; you control what you do, how you do it and when you do it. That's something to be proud of.

And never underestimate that triumph – to achieve all that, on your own, through determination and commitment, to stick with it and survive the knock-backs, and to survive. That is what business is all about.

29
Now, the end (or, actually, the beginning)

As I sat on the balcony of our apartment enjoying my last sip of red wine, I looked up at the starlit sky and the palm trees. And I thought of ideas for my latest venture, its challenges and solutions. Here I am again, I thought to myself, on another holiday, my mind busy with another idea.

Having 'another idea' is what working for yourself is all about: that freedom to explore new ideas and possibilities when you feel like it.

Back on the balcony I reflected on the benefits of what I am and what I do:

! I can do whatever I want to do; I can do anything and everything. No rules and no limits.

! The only limit is my own imagination. No one to answer to but myself.

! For I've carved out a role where I put my own distinctive stamp on all I do.

! Is it tough? Yes. Is it hard work? You bet. But I can do whatever I choose.

I have what we all strive for in life:

I HAVE A CHOICE.

To choose how to work, to choose how I'm going to make a difference and to carve out my own worklife. To choose how I balance work and play, to choose whether to go to the office today or not. And, yes, even to choose what colour socks I wear.

I have joined the *scrambled up world of work*. And, in doing so, I am free!

That freedom to choose gives you the ability to edit the different elements of your life:

> 'It's like my whole work life is an algorithm pushing and pulling agendas up and down the priority list. I'm no longer a worker, I'm an editor, making real time decisions as to what must be done right now, next, tomorrow. Play and work are the same. I play, clear my head, come up with a solution for a client's problem, go to work on it, feel tired, go and play to relax. This lifestyle, if edited correctly, can only be described as damn beautiful.'

David Sloly, Digital Guru and Scrambled Up Worker

Take the *Leap!* and put all those ideas into practice.

People rarely regret what they do; rather, they regret what they don't do.

So, whatever you do…

Ditch your job
Start your own business
And set yourself free!

Go on, what are you waiting for…?

Appendix

Tales From The Frontline
Of The Scrambled Up
World Of Work

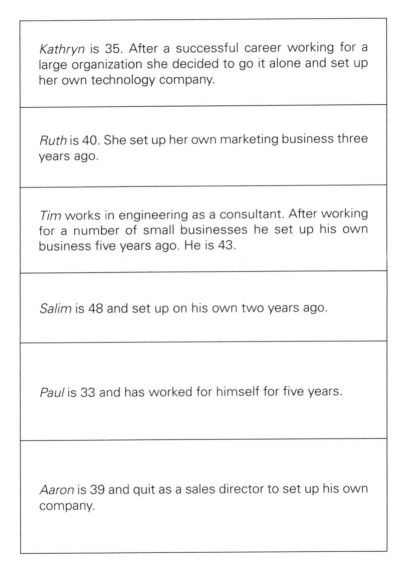

Kathryn is 35. After a successful career working for a large organization she decided to go it alone and set up her own technology company.

Ruth is 40. She set up her own marketing business three years ago.

Tim works in engineering as a consultant. After working for a number of small businesses he set up his own business five years ago. He is 43.

Salim is 48 and set up on his own two years ago.

Paul is 33 and has worked for himself for five years.

Aaron is 39 and quit as a sales director to set up his own company.

WHY DID YOU DECIDE TO TAKE THE *LEAP*?

Kathyrn: I felt there were opportunities that I was missing out on in my professional career. I felt that in order to develop my professional skills it was time to move on.

Ruth: I spotted some opportunities in my old job that I could handle if I went it alone.

Tim: I needed to control my work/life balance more; I'd tired of company politics and also I wanted to spend more time with my children.

Salim: I was 46 and found that no company was willing to pay what I saw as the appropriate salary for my experience; they were choosing younger candidates. Having to go forward and find a better way to make a living there was simply no other option than to take the *Leap!*.

Paul: I wanted to be my own boss and return to the sort of work I wanted to do.

Aaron: I had built a career on delivering success to my employers, growing sales targets. The company put someone else into my role without notice and my gut feeling was to say 'enough' and move on.

WHAT WAS THE CATALYST?

K: The main thought was that if I didn't do it now, I would never do it, and spend the rest of my life wondering 'what if?'

R: I had been offered a new job but it transpired to be not what was promised. I was disillusioned and thought it was time to take the *Leap!*.

T: The fact that I had recently split up with my wife meant I felt I had nothing to lose by making such a change.

S: The catalyst was simply realizing I had limited options; I wanted to be in control of my future – the only choice was to *Leap!*.

P: My friends and colleagues encouraged me to; and I had recently lost my mother so I had a spirit of 'carpe diem'. I also had some good contacts with existing colleagues who promised me work.

A: I was disillusioned with how my employers treated me after years of loyalty and dedication to them. My family life had suffered because I was working too hard and it was definitely time for a change.

WHAT'S BEEN THE GOOD THING ABOUT TAKING THE *LEAP*?

K: The freedom to make my own decisions and to try new things out.

R: It's great being your own boss with a broad variety and scope of work.

T: It's great controlling your life, some years taking ten weeks' holiday and earning excellent money when the going is good.

S: Driving to my office in the morning and knowing that I'm working for myself, investing time and money for my self, getting satisfaction and being content with the way I'm running my own business.

P: Achieving all my goals!

A: It teaches you to stop hiding behind corporate facades; to live by values and principles that you create rather than corporate values on a website that someone else has created.

WHAT SURPRISED YOU?

K: I expected the shift from being part of a large organization to managing my own time to be more difficult; it's actually been easier than I thought.

R: My self-discipline surprised me, I have found it quite easy to work at home and often start work at 7 a.m.

T: I loved how supportive everyone was, and how little bad debt I have incurred.

S: How quickly personal contacts from the past passed on jobs to us. They knew us and many of them trusted us to do a good job. That was the beginning of our business.

P: It's been great that I have survived and stayed in business for five years. That's an achievement!

A: I was surprised at how good I was at things I didn't know about. I was also surprised to see my ideas and dreams actually working out.

HOW DOES IT COMPARE WITH YOUR
'PROPER' JOB?

K: It has its own challenges – motivation is one of the biggest ones: if I don't do something, no one else will. Also in my old job I was able to keep weekends free; now I have to take the work as and when it comes in.

R: This is miles better than working for someone else!

T: It can be quite an insecure experience and isolating at times. You don't get a feeling of career advancement as such; it can be very emancipating so long as that's your main criteria for success (along with decent earnings of course!)

S: I'm more involved and it triggers more feeling of responsibility and lets you open your mind to other aspects of the business.

P: There's more freedom to work in the way that suits me; I get the financial rewards directly for a job well done and more sense of achievement. I'm also more productive working at home than in the office.

A: I'm much more excited about what I do now; you never know what's round the corner and what tomorrow will bring.

WOULD YOU GO BACK TO A 'PROPER' JOB?

K: No, for the moment I still have things to prove to myself.

R: No way, never!

T: As I get older, I may want to concentrate on doing the work rather than seeking out the work as well. That's when I may go and get a proper job again.

S: No way!

P: I'd avoid it so long as I can ensure financial stability; I'd rather stay working for myself.

A: If I saw an amazing role perhaps, but I would rather stay working for myself and grow and develop what I have achieved to date.

HOW DO YOU FIND WORKING FOR YOURSELF?

K: Working for yourself may be more stressful but it's also more rewarding. I certainly wouldn't have considered myself an 'entrepreneur' 12 months ago. But in business, 12 months is a long time.

R: I have much more self-belief, a greater confidence to achieve. It's much more 'me'.

T: I have a much more pragmatic view on business

S: I feel more responsibility and dip deeper into challenges.

P: Generally work is not a chore; I get more satisfaction so feel happier.

A: I like the feeling of self-sufficiency, the essence I have to survive and provide for myself and my family.

Index